Mometrix TEST PREPARATION

Georgia Literature and Composition EOC Success Strategies

I0878898

Dear Future Exam Success Story

First of all, **THANK YOU** for purchasing Mometrix study materials!

Second, congratulations! You are one of the few determined test-takers who are committed to doing whatever it takes to excel on your exam. **You have come to the right place.** We developed these study materials with one goal in mind: to deliver you the information you need in a format that's concise and easy to use.

In addition to optimizing your guide for the content of the test, we've outlined our recommended steps for breaking down the preparation process into small, attainable goals so you can make sure you stay on track.

We've also analyzed the entire test-taking process, identifying the most common pitfalls and showing how you can overcome them and be ready for any curveball the test throws you.

Standardized testing is one of the biggest obstacles on your road to success, which only increases the importance of doing well in the high-pressure, high-stakes environment of test day. Your results on this test could have a significant impact on your future, and this guide provides the information and practical advice to help you achieve your full potential on test day.

Your success is our success

We would love to hear from you! If you would like to share the story of your exam success or if you have any questions or comments in regard to our products, please contact us at **800-673-8175** or **support@mometrix.com**.

Thanks again for your business and we wish you continued success!

Sincerely,
The Mometrix Test Preparation Team

Written and edited by the Mometrix Test Preparation Team
Printed in the United States of America

TABLE OF CONTENTS

Introduction

Thank you for purchasing this resource! You have made the choice to prepare yourself for a test that could have a huge impact on your future, and this guide is designed to help you be fully ready for test day. Obviously, it's important to have a solid understanding of the test material, but you also need to be prepared for the unique environment and stressors of the test, so that you can perform to the best of your abilities.

For this purpose, the first section that appears in this guide is the **Success Strategies**. We've devoted countless hours to meticulously researching what works and what doesn't, and we've boiled down our findings to the most impactful steps you can take to improve your performance on the test. We start at the beginning with study planning and move through the preparation process, all the way to the testing strategies that will help you get the most out of what you know when you're finally sitting in front of the test.

We recommend that you start preparing for your test as far in advance as possible. However, if you've bought this guide as a last-minute study resource and only have a few days before your test, we recommend that you skip over the first two Success Strategies since they address a long-term study plan.

If you struggle with **test anxiety**, we strongly encourage you to check out our recommendations for how you can overcome it. Test anxiety is a formidable foe, but it can be beaten, and we want to make sure you have the tools you need to defeat it.

Strategy #1 – Plan Big, Study Small

There's a lot riding on your performance. If you want to ace this test, you're going to need to keep your skills sharp and the material fresh in your mind. You need a plan that lets you review everything you need to know while still fitting in your schedule. We'll break this strategy down into three categories.

Information Organization

Start with the information you already have: the official test outline. From this, you can make a complete list of all the concepts you need to cover before the test. Organize these concepts into groups that can be studied together, and create a list of any related vocabulary you need to learn so you can brush up on any difficult terms. You'll want to keep this vocabulary list handy once you actually start studying since you may need to add to it along the way.

Time Management

Once you have your set of study concepts, decide how to spread them out over the time you have left before the test. Break your study plan into small, clear goals so you have a manageable task for each day and know exactly what you're doing. Then just focus on one small step at a time. When you manage your time this way, you don't need to spend hours at a time studying. Studying a small block of content for a short period each day helps you retain information better and avoid stressing over how much you have left to do. You can relax knowing that you have a plan to cover everything in time. In order for this strategy to be effective though, you have to start studying early and stick to your schedule. Avoid the exhaustion and futility that comes from last-minute cramming!

Study Environment

The environment you study in has a big impact on your learning. Studying in a coffee shop, while probably more enjoyable, is not likely to be as fruitful as studying in a quiet room. It's important to keep distractions to a minimum. You're only planning to study for a short block of time, so make the most of it. Don't pause to check your phone or get up to find a snack. It's also important to **avoid multitasking**. Research has consistently shown that multitasking will make your studying dramatically less effective. Your study area should also be comfortable and well-lit so you don't have the distraction of straining your eyes or sitting on an uncomfortable chair.

The time of day you study is also important. You want to be rested and alert. Don't wait until just before bedtime. Study when you'll be most likely to comprehend and remember. Even better, if you know what time of day your test will be, set that time aside for study. That way your brain will be used to working on that subject at that specific time and you'll have a better chance of recalling information.

Finally, it can be helpful to team up with others who are studying for the same test. Your actual studying should be done in as isolated an environment as possible, but the work of organizing the information and setting up the study plan can be divided up. In between study sessions, you can discuss with your teammates the concepts that you're all studying and quiz each other on the details. Just be sure that your teammates are as serious about the test as you are. If you find that your study time is being replaced with social time, you might need to find a new team.

Strategy #2 – Make Your Studying Count

You're devoting a lot of time and effort to preparing for this test, so you want to be absolutely certain it will pay off. This means doing more than just reading the content and hoping you can remember it on test day. It's important to make every minute of study count. There are two main areas you can focus on to make your studying count.

Retention

It doesn't matter how much time you study if you can't remember the material. You need to make sure you are retaining the concepts. To check your retention of the information you're learning, try recalling it at later times with minimal prompting. Try carrying around flashcards and glance at one or two from time to time or ask a friend who's also studying for the test to quiz you.

To enhance your retention, look for ways to put the information into practice so that you can apply it rather than simply recalling it. If you're using the information in practical ways, it will be much easier to remember. Similarly, it helps to solidify a concept in your mind if you're not only reading it to yourself but also explaining it to someone else. Ask a friend to let you teach them about a concept you're a little shaky on (or speak aloud to an imaginary audience if necessary). As you try to summarize, define, give examples, and answer your friend's questions, you'll understand the concepts better and they will stay with you longer. Finally, step back for a big picture view and ask yourself how each piece of information fits with the whole subject. When you link the different concepts together and see them working together as a whole, it's easier to remember the individual components.

Finally, practice showing your work on any multi-step problems, even if you're just studying. Writing out each step you take to solve a problem will help solidify the process in your mind, and you'll be more likely to remember it during the test.

Modality

Modality simply refers to the means or method by which you study. Choosing a study modality that fits your own individual learning style is crucial. No two people learn best in exactly the same way, so it's important to know your strengths and use them to your advantage.

For example, if you learn best by visualization, focus on visualizing a concept in your mind and draw an image or a diagram. Try color-coding your notes, illustrating them, or creating symbols that will trigger your mind to recall a learned concept. If you learn best by hearing or discussing information, find a study partner who learns the same way or read aloud to yourself. Think about how to put the information in your own words. Imagine that you are giving a lecture on the topic and record yourself so you can listen to it later.

For any learning style, flashcards can be helpful. Organize the information so you can take advantage of spare moments to review. Underline key words or phrases. Use different colors for different categories. Mnemonic devices (such as creating a short list in which every item starts with the same letter) can also help with retention. Find what works best for you and use it to store the information in your mind most effectively and easily.

Strategy #3 – Practice the Right Way

Your success on test day depends not only on how many hours you put into preparing, but also on whether you prepared the right way. It's good to check along the way to see if your studying is paying off. One of the most effective ways to do this is by taking practice tests to evaluate your progress. Practice tests are useful because they show exactly where you need to improve. Every time you take a practice test, pay special attention to these three groups of questions:

- The questions you got wrong
- The questions you had to guess on, even if you guessed right
- The questions you found difficult or slow to work through

This will show you exactly what your weak areas are, and where you need to devote more study time. Ask yourself why each of these questions gave you trouble. Was it because you didn't understand the material? Was it because you didn't remember the vocabulary? Do you need more repetitions on this type of question to build speed and confidence? Dig into those questions and figure out how you can strengthen your weak areas as you go back to review the material.

Additionally, many practice tests have a section explaining the answer choices. It can be tempting to read the explanation and think that you now have a good understanding of the concept. However, an explanation likely only covers part of the question's broader context. Even if the explanation makes perfect sense, **go back and investigate** every concept related to the question until you're positive you have a thorough understanding.

As you go along, keep in mind that the practice test is just that: practice. Memorizing these questions and answers will not be very helpful on the actual test because it is unlikely to have any of the same exact questions. If you only know the right answers to the sample questions, you won't be prepared for the real thing. **Study the concepts** until you understand them fully, and then you'll be able to answer any question that shows up on the test.

It's important to wait on the practice tests until you're ready. If you take a test on your first day of study, you may be overwhelmed by the amount of material covered and how much you need to learn. Work up to it gradually.

On test day, you'll need to be prepared for answering questions, managing your time, and using the test-taking strategies you've learned. It's a lot to balance, like a mental marathon that will have a big impact on your future. Like training for a marathon, you'll need to start slowly and work your way up. When test day arrives, you'll be ready.

Start with the strategies you've read in the first two Success Strategies—plan your course and study in the way that works best for you. If you have time, consider using multiple study resources to get different approaches to the same concepts. It can be helpful to see difficult concepts from more than one angle. Then find a good source for practice tests. Many times, the test website will suggest potential study resources or provide sample tests.

Practice Test Strategy

If you're able to find at least three practice tests, we recommend this strategy:

Untimed and Open-Book Practice

Take the first test with no time constraints and with your notes and study guide handy. Take your time and focus on applying the strategies you've learned.

Timed and Open-Book Practice

Take the second practice test open-book as well, but set a timer and practice pacing yourself to finish in time.

Timed and Closed-Book Practice

Take any other practice tests as if it were test day. Set a timer and put away your study materials. Sit at a table or desk in a quiet room, imagine yourself at the testing center, and answer questions as quickly and accurately as possible.

Keep repeating timed and closed-book tests on a regular basis until you run out of practice tests or it's time for the actual test. Your mind will be ready for the schedule and stress of test day, and you'll be able to focus on recalling the material you've learned.

Strategy #4 – Pace Yourself

Once you're fully prepared for the material on the test, your biggest challenge on test day will be managing your time. Just knowing that the clock is ticking can make you panic even if you have plenty of time left. Work on pacing yourself so you can build confidence against the time constraints of the exam. Pacing is a difficult skill to master, especially in a high-pressure environment, so **practice is vital**.

Set time expectations for your pace based on how much time is available. For example, if a section has 60 questions and the time limit is 30 minutes, you know you have to average 30 seconds or less per question in order to answer them all. Although 30 seconds is the hard limit, set 25 seconds per question as your goal, so you reserve extra time to spend on harder questions. When you budget extra time for the harder questions, you no longer have any reason to stress when those questions take longer to answer.

Don't let this time expectation distract you from working through the test at a calm, steady pace, but keep it in mind so you don't spend too much time on any one question. Recognize that taking extra time on one question you don't understand may keep you from answering two that you do understand later in the test. If your time limit for a question is up and you're still not sure of the answer, mark it and move on, and come back to it later if the time and the test format allow. If the testing format doesn't allow you to return to earlier questions, just make an educated guess; then put it out of your mind and move on.

On the easier questions, be careful not to rush. It may seem wise to hurry through them so you have more time for the challenging ones, but it's not worth missing one if you know the concept and just didn't take the time to read the question fully. Work efficiently but make sure you understand the question and have looked at all of the answer choices, since more than one may seem right at first.

Even if you're paying attention to the time, you may find yourself a little behind at some point. You should speed up to get back on track, but do so wisely. Don't panic; just take a few seconds less on each question until you're caught up. Don't guess without thinking, but do look through the answer choices and eliminate any you know are wrong. If you can get down to two choices, it is often worthwhile to guess from those. Once you've chosen an answer, move on and don't dwell on any that you skipped or had to hurry through. If a question was taking too long, chances are it was one of the harder ones, so you weren't as likely to get it right anyway.

On the other hand, if you find yourself getting ahead of schedule, it may be beneficial to slow down a little. The more quickly you work, the more likely you are to make a careless mistake that will affect your score. You've budgeted time for each question, so don't be afraid to spend that time. Practice an efficient but careful pace to get the most out of the time you have.

Test-Taking Strategies

This section contains a list of test-taking strategies that you may find helpful as you work through the test. By taking what you know and applying logical thought, you can maximize your chances of answering any question correctly!

It is very important to realize that every question is different and every person is different: no single strategy will work on every question, and no single strategy will work for every person. That's why we've included all of them here, so you can try them out and determine which ones work best for different types of questions and which ones work best for you.

Question Strategies

☑ Read Carefully

Read the question and the answer choices carefully. Don't miss the question because you misread the terms. You have plenty of time to read each question thoroughly and make sure you understand what is being asked. Yet a happy medium must be attained, so don't waste too much time. You must read carefully and efficiently.

☑ Contextual Clues

Look for contextual clues. If the question includes a word you are not familiar with, look at the immediate context for some indication of what the word might mean. Contextual clues can often give you all the information you need to decipher the meaning of an unfamiliar word. Even if you can't determine the meaning, you may be able to narrow down the possibilities enough to make a solid guess at the answer to the question.

☑ Prefixes

If you're having trouble with a word in the question or answer choices, try dissecting it. Take advantage of every clue that the word might include. Prefixes can be a huge help. Usually, they allow you to determine a basic meaning. *Pre-* means before, *post-* means after, *pro-* is positive, *de-* is negative. From prefixes, you can get an idea of the general meaning of the word and try to put it into context.

☑ Hedge Words

Watch out for critical hedge words, such as *likely, may, can, often, almost, mostly, usually, generally, rarely*, and *sometimes*. Question writers insert these hedge phrases to cover every possibility. Often an answer choice will be wrong simply because it leaves no room for exception. Be on guard for answer choices that have definitive words such as *exactly* and *always*.

☑ Switchback Words

Stay alert for *switchbacks*. These are the words and phrases frequently used to alert you to shifts in thought. The most common switchback words are *but, although*, and *however*. Others include *nevertheless, on the other hand, even though, while, in spite of, despite*, and *regardless of*. Switchback words are important to catch because they can change the direction of the question or an answer choice.

☑ FACE VALUE

When in doubt, use common sense. Accept the situation in the problem at face value. Don't read too much into it. These problems will not require you to make wild assumptions. If you have to go beyond creativity and warp time or space in order to have an answer choice fit the question, then you should move on and consider the other answer choices. These are normal problems rooted in reality. The applicable relationship or explanation may not be readily apparent, but it is there for you to figure out. Use your common sense to interpret anything that isn't clear.

Answer Choice Strategies

☑ ANSWER SELECTION

The most thorough way to pick an answer choice is to identify and eliminate wrong answers until only one is left, then confirm it is the correct answer. Sometimes an answer choice may immediately seem right, but be careful. The test writers will usually put more than one reasonable answer choice on each question, so take a second to read all of them and make sure that the other choices are not equally obvious. As long as you have time left, it is better to read every answer choice than to pick the first one that looks right without checking the others.

☑ ANSWER CHOICE FAMILIES

An answer choice family consists of two (in rare cases, three) answer choices that are very similar in construction and cannot all be true at the same time. If you see two answer choices that are direct opposites or parallels, one of them is usually the correct answer. For instance, if one answer choice says that quantity *x* increases and another either says that quantity *x* decreases (opposite) or says that quantity *y* increases (parallel), then those answer choices would fall into the same family. An answer choice that doesn't match the construction of the answer choice family is more likely to be incorrect. Most questions will not have answer choice families, but when they do appear, you should be prepared to recognize them.

☑ ELIMINATE ANSWERS

Eliminate answer choices as soon as you realize they are wrong, but make sure you consider all possibilities. If you are eliminating answer choices and realize that the last one you are left with is also wrong, don't panic. Start over and consider each choice again. There may be something you missed the first time that you will realize on the second pass.

☑ AVOID FACT TRAPS

Don't be distracted by an answer choice that is factually true but doesn't answer the question. You are looking for the choice that answers the question. Stay focused on what the question is asking for so you don't accidentally pick an answer that is true but incorrect. Always go back to the question and make sure the answer choice you've selected actually answers the question and is not merely a true statement.

☑ EXTREME STATEMENTS

In general, you should avoid answers that put forth extreme actions as standard practice or proclaim controversial ideas as established fact. An answer choice that states the "process should be used in certain situations, if…" is much more likely to be correct than one that states the "process should be discontinued completely." The first is a calm rational statement and doesn't even make a definitive, uncompromising stance, using a hedge word *if* to provide wiggle room, whereas the second choice is far more extreme.

☑ BENCHMARK

As you read through the answer choices and you come across one that seems to answer the question well, mentally select that answer choice. This is not your final answer, but it's the one that will help you evaluate the other answer choices. The one that you selected is your benchmark or standard for judging each of the other answer choices. Every other answer choice must be compared to your benchmark. That choice is correct until proven otherwise by another answer choice beating it. If you find a better answer, then that one becomes your new benchmark. Once you've decided that no other choice answers the question as well as your benchmark, you have your final answer.

☑ PREDICT THE ANSWER

Before you even start looking at the answer choices, it is often best to try to predict the answer. When you come up with the answer on your own, it is easier to avoid distractions and traps because you will know exactly what to look for. The right answer choice is unlikely to be word-for-word what you came up with, but it should be a close match. Even if you are confident that you have the right answer, you should still take the time to read each option before moving on.

General Strategies

☑ TOUGH QUESTIONS

If you are stumped on a problem or it appears too hard or too difficult, don't waste time. Move on! Remember though, if you can quickly check for obviously incorrect answer choices, your chances of guessing correctly are greatly improved. Before you completely give up, at least try to knock out a couple of possible answers. Eliminate what you can and then guess at the remaining answer choices before moving on.

☑ CHECK YOUR WORK

Since you will probably not know every term listed and the answer to every question, it is important that you get credit for the ones that you do know. Don't miss any questions through careless mistakes. If at all possible, try to take a second to look back over your answer selection and make sure you've selected the correct answer choice and haven't made a costly careless mistake (such as marking an answer choice that you didn't mean to mark). This quick double check should more than pay for itself in caught mistakes for the time it costs.

☑ PACE YOURSELF

It's easy to be overwhelmed when you're looking at a page full of questions; your mind is confused and full of random thoughts, and the clock is ticking down faster than you would like. Calm down and maintain the pace that you have set for yourself. Especially as you get down to the last few minutes of the test, don't let the small numbers on the clock make you panic. As long as you are on track by monitoring your pace, you are guaranteed to have time for each question.

☑ DON'T RUSH

It is very easy to make errors when you are in a hurry. Maintaining a fast pace in answering questions is pointless if it makes you miss questions that you would have gotten right otherwise. Test writers like to include distracting information and wrong answers that seem right. Taking a little extra time to avoid careless mistakes can make all the difference in your test score. Find a pace that allows you to be confident in the answers that you select.

⊘ KEEP MOVING

Panicking will not help you pass the test, so do your best to stay calm and keep moving. Taking deep breaths and going through the answer elimination steps you practiced can help to break through a stress barrier and keep your pace.

Final Notes

The combination of a solid foundation of content knowledge and the confidence that comes from practicing your plan for applying that knowledge is the key to maximizing your performance on test day. As your foundation of content knowledge is built up and strengthened, you'll find that the strategies included in this chapter become more and more effective in helping you quickly sift through the distractions and traps of the test to isolate the correct answer.

Now that you're preparing to move forward into the test content chapters of this book, be sure to keep your goal in mind. As you read, think about how you will be able to apply this information on the test. If you've already seen sample questions for the test and you have an idea of the question format and style, try to come up with questions of your own that you can answer based on what you're reading. This will give you valuable practice applying your knowledge in the same ways you can expect to on test day.

Good luck and good studying!

Reading and Vocabulary

Reading Literature

Context

When you come across an unfamiliar word or phrase when you are reading, you can use context clues to make a guess as to the meaning of the word. Look at the whole sentence that contains the word, not just the words immediately before and after the unfamiliar word. You may even need to use context clues in the paragraph as a whole. Often, you can find a clue in the sentence before or after the one with the unfamiliar word. Context clues can be descriptions, synonyms, antonyms, and definitions. In addition, the tone of the sentence may help you determine the meaning. Once you take a guess at the meaning, reread the sentence replacing the unfamiliar word with your guess. Ask yourself if the sentence makes sense. If it makes sense, continue reading based on your assumption.

Multiple Meaning Words

Some words are spelled exactly the same but have different meaning in different contexts. You need to use the context of the situation to determine the correct meaning. The word *degree* has at least three different meanings depending on the situation in which the word is used. 1.) A *degree* is the incremental measurement of temperature. 2.) A *degree* is a title awarded upon graduation. 3.) Finally, *degree* can mean the extent or amount of something. Here are three different sentences using the word *degree*:

1. You probably don't notice a difference when the temperature rises one *degree*.
2. The employer is only willing to hire someone with a college *degree* in mathematics.
3. It was hard to tell the *degree* to which he really cared about the outcome.

Multiple meaning words are words spelled exactly the same but have different meanings in different contexts. The context of the situation must be used to determine the correct meaning in each case. Often, these words can be used as either a noun or a verb and their grammatical usage determines the meaning. The word *might* has two different meanings, depending on how it is used in the sentence. *Might* as a verb indicates the possibility that something "may occur" while *might* as a noun means "strength" or "power." Here are two different sentences using *might* in each way.

1. He *might* join us at the movies tomorrow night.
2. The warrior pushed with all of his *might*.

Character Analysis

When analyzing a character, you should pay attention to the character's physical traits, thoughts, feelings, attitudes, and motivations. Physical traits include any description of how the character appears. This can include hair and eye color, height, and clothing, for example. The characters thoughts, feelings, and attitudes include his or her ideas about a certain topic or another character. The character's motivations are the reasons why he or she behaves a certain way. For example, in a mystery novel, the protagonist may act in a deceitful way toward a suspect, but the motivation for doing so may be to gain information and uncover the truth. This lets the reader understand that even though the character acts in a deceitful way, he or she is not a bad person, and it allows the reader to better understand the character.

Idiom

An idiom is a type of figurative language. An idiomatic phrase has a meaning other than the literal meaning of the words in the phrase. Authors use idioms and other examples of figurative language to add color to their writing and make it more interesting for the reader. Common phrases like "kick the bucket" and "bent out of shape" are examples of idioms. The phrase "kick the bucket" does not actually mean that a person uses his foot to knock over a bucket, but instead means he dies. Likewise, when a person gets "bent out of shape," his shape does not actually change; rather, it means he is worried about something.

Prefixes and suffixes

Prefixes are parts of words that, when added to the beginning of a root word, form a new word. The prefix *hyper-* means "over" or "very." The root of the word *hypersensitive* is *sensitive* which means "thin-skinned" or "touchy." Using knowledge of the prefix and the root, a person could determine that the word *hypersensitive* means "overly touchy" or "very thin-skinned." This approximate definition based on knowledge of prefixes and root words gives an accurate meaning of the word *hypersensitive.*

Suffixes are parts of words that, when added to the end of a root word, form a new word. The suffix *-ic* means "having to do with." The root, *dynam-* means "power." Using this knowledge, an approximate meaning of the word *dynamic* is "having to do with power." The literal definition is "full of energy" or "characterized by vigorous activity." In this case, the approximate definition is close to the literal definition and could help you understand the word enough to use it to understand the rest of the paragraph in which it is used.

Glossary

A glossary is a list of terms and their definitions that can be found at the back of certain types of books, such as textbooks or reference books. A glossary does not have the definitions of all words, like a dictionary, but instead gives the definitions of the important terms within that particular book which are either uncommon or newly introduced. One may use a glossary when reading a book about economics or a chapter in a science textbook, for example, to define some of the technical terms within the text.

Allusion

An allusion is an un-cited but recognizable reference to something else. Authors use language to make allusions to places, events, artwork, and other books in order to make their own text richer. For example, an author may allude to a very important text in order to make his own text seem more important. Martin Luther King, Jr. started his "I Have a Dream" speech by saying "Five score years ago…" This is a clear allusion to President Abraham Lincoln's "Gettysburg Address" and served to remind people of the significance of the event. An author may allude to a place to ground his text or make a cultural reference to make readers feel included. There are many reasons that authors make allusions.

Myth, legend, and tall tale

A *myth* is a traditional story that serves to explain a world view or belief of a particular people. It is usually a symbolic narrative that deals with the origin of the universe and the other worldly powers that control humans. A *legend*, on the other hand, is a story that is usually handed down from one generation to another by means of oral storytelling. They are stories about people, places, and events in the past and have an historical context. A *tall tale* is a story with unbelievable or exaggerated elements that is told as if these elements were true. The exaggeration usually serves to underscore some important lesson that the storyteller is trying to teach.

Setting and Time Frame

A literary text has both a setting and time frame. A setting is the place in which the story as a whole is set. The time frame is the period in which the story is set. This may be a historical period or that the story is set over the course of a single day. Both setting and time frame are relevant to a text's meaning because they help the reader place the story in time and space. An author uses setting and time frame to anchor a text, create a mood, and enhance its meaning; helping a reader understand why a character acts the way he does, or why certain events in the story are important. The setting impacts the plot and character motivations, while the time frame helps place the story in chronological context.

Analyze the Relevance of Setting to the Text's Meaning in the Following Excerpt

We said there warn't no home like a raft, after all. Other places do seem so cramped up and smothery, but a raft don't. You feel mighty free and easy and comfortable on a raft.

This excerpt from The Adventures of Huckleberry Finn by Mark Twain reveals information about the setting of the book. By understanding that the main character, Huckleberry Finn, lives on a raft, the reader can place the story on a river, in this case, the Mississippi River in the South before the Civil War. The information about the setting also gives the reader clues about the character of Huck Finn: he clearly values independence and freedom and he likes the outdoors. The information about the setting in the quote helps the reader to better understand the rest of the text.

Connecting Literature to Historical and Current Events

Comprehensive readers are readers who use a number of different skills to fully understand a text. One way to better understand a text, and literature as a whole, is to make connections. Comprehensive readers make connections between the text and themselves, different texts, and even the real world. By connecting a text to historical and current events, the reader does not see the text as the only information on the given subject. The reader uses both historical and current events to better understand the text and place it in context of similarities and differences of actions and opinions.

Comic Relief

Comic relief is the use of comedy by an author to break up a dramatic or tragic scene and infuse it with a bit of lightheartedness. In William Shakespeare's Hamlet, two gravediggers digging the grave for Ophelia share a joke while they work. The death and burial of Ophelia are tragic moments that directly follow each other. Shakespeare uses an instance of comedy to break up the tragedy and give his audience a bit of a break from the tragic drama. In general, authors use comic relief so that their work will not be overwhelmingly dark and depressing. Often, authors will use comedy to parallel what is happening in the tragic scenes.

Chronological Order

A biography is the story of someone's life or an important and more specific part of it. Chronological order indicates the telling of events in the order they happened. When writing a biography, it generally makes sense to use chronological order to tell the significant events of a person's life in the order they occurred. This helps the reader to better understand the motive for the person's behavior, as they might have acted as they did, due to an earlier event. It also helps the reader place significant events in order (i.e., which prize the person won first, second, etc.) If a biography contained the significant events in a person's life, but was not written chronologically, the reader would have a hard time understanding the trajectory of the person's life.

INFERENCE

An inference is a conclusion that the reader makes using clues in the text. In a work of literature, there are things that the author does not explicitly mention, but rather hints at. The reader needs to connect the dots of these clues to draw a conclusion, or an inference. An inference is different from making a guess because it is based on evidence. The reader uses specific textual evidence to make the inference. For example, an author might mention that a character has a messy room and papers falling out of his binder. The reader can infer that the character is sloppy and disorganized, even though the author does not explicitly state this fact.

When readers read comprehensively, they link clues from the text together to make inferences, or conclusions based on information in the text. In a work of fiction, there are things that the author does not explicitly mention, but rather hints at. The reader needs to connect the dots of these clues and hints to draw a conclusion. Making predictions is one kind of inference; based on what has happened so far, the reader is inferring what will happen later in the book. When a reader does not base his ideas on the actual clues in the text, he is not making an inference, but rather, is simply having a thought connected in some way to the book.

NEWSPAPER ARTICLES, SHORT STORIES, AND ADVERTISEMENTS

When authors write, it is always with a purpose. There are four main purposes: to inform, to entertain, to describe, and to persuade. A newspaper article is most often a factual account of something that occurred, written to inform readers about the event. A short story is fiction; it may be sad, funny, or even uplifting; but regardless of the emotion it brings out, fiction is written to entertain. People read fiction to escape their lives and be entertained. Advertisements, whether in print, on television, or Internet ads, are written to convince the reader to do or buy something. The purpose of advertisements is to persuade the reader to do something.

PERSUASIVE TECHNIQUE

THIS MOVIE IS THE GREATEST EVER! YOU SHOULD COME SEE IT AND YOU SHOULD BRING ALL OF YOUR FRIENDS. YOU WILL HAVE A GREAT TIME! GUARANTEED!

This advertisement is for a movie. The persuasive technique being used is that of glittering generalities. The tone of the wording and the use of exclamation points makes the movie sound fun and appeals to the reader's love of hanging out with friends, but the advertisement contains no specific information about the movie. What is the movie about that makes it so great? There is no actual meaning to these words because the reader does not know what the movie is about, but it does appeal to the reader's emotions and love of fun

WRITING THE SAME STORY DIFFERENTLY

Just like when speaking, one needs to keep their audience and purpose in mind when writing. For an informal audience, like a friend, the document can be written in an informal way, using contractions and slang and less strict grammar. The purpose might be to simply tell an entertaining story. When writing for a school assignment, on the other hand, the document must be written in a formal manner. Vocabulary should be at a higher level and sentences should be varied and interesting. The purpose of writing for a school assignment is to show the teacher how much one knows. In addition, one might also highlight different aspects of the same event for different audiences.

IDENTIFYING CONFLICT

The conflict in a plot is the main problem. The typical plot starts with background information and then has rising action. This section is generally where the conflict, or problem, is introduced. The climax is when the conflict is most pronounced. The falling action and resolution provide the solution to the problem. There are three main types of conflict in literature: man versus man, man versus nature, and man versus self. In man versus man conflicts, the conflict is often resolved by the two people coming to some sort of agreement. In man versus nature conflicts, the conflict is often resolved by man coming to grips with some aspect of nature. In man versus self conflicts, the conflict is resolved by the character growing or coming to an understanding of himself.

Evocative Words and Rhythm

The terms *evocative words* and *rhythm* are both related to the melodies of literary language, most likely poetry. Evocative words are words that bring something to mind, usually an emotion. Rhythm is the beat of the words. Evocative words and rhythms add layers to a text. A text is more than just the words on the page, but also the way those words sound, and how those sounds impact the reader. The insistent drum beat of short, choppy words evokes a different feeling from that of long, flowing sentences. Evocative words and rhythm both help the reader make connections and feel the tone of the text.

Poetic Rhythm

"I hear the sound I love, the sound of the human voice;
I hear all sounds running together, combined, fused or following;
Sounds of the city, and sounds out of the city—sounds of the day and night;
Talkative young ones to those that like them—the loud laugh of work-people at their meals"

Poetry is meant to be read aloud, or recited, and listened to. Poets use rhythm to give their poems a melody or cadence. Rhythm is the stress and flow of words in a poem. Certain words and syllables are meant to be read with more emphasis than others. Poets use stressed and unstressed syllables of words to give their poems a melodic sound. One way poets develop rhythm is by the repetition of certain words. In the above example, Walt Whitman uses repetition of the word "sound" to develop the rhythm of the piece.

By the shore of Gitchie Gumee,
By the shining Big-Sea-Water,
At the doorway of his wigwam,
In the pleasant Summer morning,
Hiawatha stood and waited.

Poetry is meant to be read aloud and listened to. Poets use rhythm to give their poems melody. Rhythm is the beat of the words in a poem. Poets use stressed and unstressed syllables of words to give their poems melody and rhythm. In the above example, Henry Wadsworth Longfellow stresses the initial syllable in the line, tapering off at the end. This serves to make the reader want to keep reading the next line, and the next line.

Encyclopedia Entries, Novels, and Television Commercials

Authors always write with a purpose, the four main purposes being: to inform, to entertain, to describe, and to persuade. An encyclopedia entry is a factual account of something written to inform readers about the topic of the entry. A novel is a type of fiction that may be sad, funny, or uplifting. Regardless of the emotion it brings out, fiction is written to entertain. People read fiction to escape their lives and be entertained. Television commercials are advertisements and are written to persuade the reader to do or buy something.

Objective Summary of a Passage

A summary must include the main ideas of a passage as well as the important details that support the main idea. It should be more than a general statement about what a passage is about. It should include vital events and other details that make the story unique and memorable. In order to make the summary objective, you must make sure to reflect what the passage is about. A summary puts the information in a short form. That is how summarizing is different from paraphrasing. Paraphrasing rewords the main idea and supporting ideas in greater detail; summaries do not. Summaries allow the reader to remember the main points of a passage and the important details.

Explicit Information

Explicit information is the information that is found in a passage or story. This information can include facts, descriptions, and statements about the characters, setting, or events in a story. Explicit information is not suggested or hinted at; it is definite because it is stated right in the passage. Explicit information takes many shapes; in a description it might be that "Tom was taller than his brother." In dialogue it could be, "I have never been to Texas before." Or it could be found in an event: "Charles hit his head on the bottom of the swimming pool." Explicit information is often used as supporting evidence when making an inference.

Order of Events and Character Introduction

The way in which an author chooses to order the events of or introduce characters in a story has a strong effect on it. Most stories are told in chronological order; one event occurs after another. But, an author can influence the development of a story by placing one event out of order to emphasize its importance. Another technique used by some authors is a flashback, in which time changes from the present to the past. When it comes to introducing characters, authors have a great deal of latitude. Authors often introduce the most important characters first so that the reader will have time to get acquainted with the characters' past and present situations. Readers are often influenced by the author's feelings toward a particular character, which often have an effect on how a character is introduced.

Fresh and Engaging Language

One way to get a reader's attention and hold it is to use language that is fresh and engaging. Using a personal point of view is a good way to accomplish this. You should try to generate excitement by using a different perspective. Always avoid clichés—they will come across as stale and worn out. Learning editing skills is useful; it will help you eliminate unnecessary portions of a text. Use a dictionary and a thesaurus to locate the words you are looking for, and analyze the words to determine how a reader might perceive them. Finally, read your passage aloud to see how it sounds.

Understatement and Irony

Many authors enjoy using a sense of irony or understatement as they write a story. Both techniques distance the writer from the characters and the events of a story. In either case, the reader must read between the lines to figure out what the author is actually getting at and what his or her point of view actually is. Understatement can be used as a humorous vehicle, allowing the author to comment on what is happening without being deeply emotionally invested in it. Irony allows the author to make a statement about what is really occurring without openly stating it. When reading a text, be sure to look for any underlying meaning that an author might be trying to convey. An initial reading of a text may not be enough to discern its true intended meaning. The way an author talks about what is happening often conveys that author's viewpoint of the events.

Satire and Sarcasm

Satire exposes the follies, foibles, and traditions of society, and is often humorous. A satire critiques the pretensions of powerful people in society. While criticism is intended, it is not overt, but rather implied. Mark Twain often employed satire to make a comment about the society in which his characters lived. Sarcasm is a type of humor that is meant to be insulting. Satire may employ the literary technique of irony, which is the tension between what is expected and what actually happens. Sarcasm is a sharp, bitter comment or remark that may or may not utilize understatement. It is an obvious criticism, and does not have the sophistication or creativity of satire, which is usually associated with an entire work. Sarcasm is usually limited to a comment.

Timeless Story

The story of a young man and woman falling in love and coming to a tragic end has been told over and over, and it represents a universal theme in literature. It was originally told by the Roman writer Ovid in his play *Pyramus and Thisbe*, which is a story of forbidden love. In modern times, a musical with a plot similar to *Romeo and Juliet* is *West Side Story*, which was in fact based on Shakespeare's play. It's important to note, however, that the theme was explored even before Shakespeare wrote his tragedy. Universal themes are found throughout literature. Even the Disney movie *Lady and the Tramp* has elements of the story of ill-fated love that is recounted in *Romeo and Juliet*.

Ways in Which *Antigone* by the Greek Writer Sophocles Is Related to Henry David Thoreau's Essay "Civil Disobedience"

They are related because they share a universal theme of rebelliousness against laws that are unjust. Much of literature contains universal themes that repeat situations and ideals that humans live by. The fact that Antigone went against Creon shows that she had moral courage; the same is true of Thoreau, who argued against laws that were unjust. Even though *Antigone* is a play and was written long ago, it still relates to Thoreau's essay, which was written in the 19th century. Universal themes are timeless and are often repeated, but the context in which they are presented is affected by the times in which they are written.

Henry David Thoreau and Nathaniel Hawthorne

Thoreau was part of the Transcendental Movement that was awakening during the 19th century. It held that nature was a vital part of the human experience. Unlike the Puritanical viewpoint that people had little control over their destiny, the Transcendentalists believed that humans could choose their destiny. Thoreau was writing from this viewpoint, while Hawthorne was more concerned with the Puritanical legacy, which allowed little room for change or imagination. His books were a comment on this strict background, while Thoreau's essays were an exploration of a new world. Even though they wrote during the same century, their works represented different understandings of man's position in the universe.

Upton Sinclair's Novel *The Jungle* and John Steinbeck's Novel *The Grapes of Wrath*

These authors wrote about poor people in difficult situations; they were both concerned about social problems. This is a common theme of early 20th century literature, when the concept of helping the poor worker was just being introduced. One writer spoke of an immigrant family. The other based his novel on a migrant family. They would have had a lot in common, since both families were without roots. This theme is typical of the literature of the early 20th century, when so many immigrants were pouring into the United States. It was also timely because there were few laws restricting the kind of work that migrants could do

Reading and Comprehending a Wide Variety of Texts

The reasons why it is important for a student to be able to comprehend a wide variety of texts by the end of the 12th grade are manifold. This background will give the student a great advantage in terms of achieving success in school and the business world. Being widely read ensures greater knowledge of the world, helps a student become well-versed in cultural differences, and also gives the student a chance to develop his or her vocabulary and ability to express her or himself. Ultimately, having read a large number of different literary books will educate the student in many fields, and will help her or him become confident in our ever-complicated world, where communication is vital.

Question Scanning

On standardized tests, the reading comprehension section will generally contain a paragraph followed by a series of questions. Students may find it helpful to read each of the questions before reading the paragraph. This will alert the student to the specific details they should look for while reading. While reading the paragraph, the student will discover that the answers to the questions are more obvious. When answers do not readily appear in the course of reading, it is useful to reread the question and carefully consider each possible answer choice. Scanning questions before reading a paragraph can also provide a basic idea of the content of the article. For example, if all of the questions deal with pacemakers, the student can expect an article about that topic. Students should also pay attention to the nature of the questions. For example, a question may be general or specific. Questions that ask for names or dates indicate that the student should note these details as they read.

Topics and Main Ideas

One of the most important skills in reading comprehension is the identification of topics and main ideas. There is a subtle difference between these two features. The *topic* is the subject of a text, or what the text is about. The *main idea*, on the other hand, is the most important point being made by the author. The topic is usually expressed in few words, while the main idea often needs a full sentence to be completely defined. As an example, a short passage might have the topic of *penguins* and the main idea *Penguins are different from other birds in many ways.* In most nonfiction writing, the topic and the main idea will be stated directly, often in a sentence at the very beginning or end of the text. However, there are cases in which the reader must figure out an unstated topic or main idea. One way to approach this process is to read every sentence of the text, and try to come up with an overarching idea that is supported by each of those sentences.

Supporting Details

Supporting details are crucial to a story. These details allow the reader to "see" a character or scene in their mind. Supporting details may include descriptions of the weather, the color of a character's eyes or hair, or the sounds that a character hears. All of these details help readers understand the character as a person. Supporting details also add interest to a story. Readers must be able to distinguish between a main idea and supporting details. Supporting details are usually mentioned only once; they help create or develop the main idea.

Themes

Themes are seldom expressed directly in a text, so they can be difficult to identify. A theme is an issue, an idea, or a question raised by the text. For instance, a theme of William Shakespeare's *Hamlet* is indecision, as the title character explores his own psyche and the results of his failure to make bold choices. A great work of literature may have many themes, and the reader is justified in identifying any for which he or she can find support. One common characteristic of themes is that they raise more questions than they answer. In a good piece of fiction, the author is not always trying to convince the reader, but may instead be trying to elevate the reader's perspective and encourage him to consider the themes more deeply. When reading, one can identify themes by constantly asking what general issues the text is addressing. A good way to evaluate an author's approach to a theme is to begin reading with a question in mind (for example, how does this text approach the theme of love?) and then look for evidence in the text that addresses that question.

Prior Knowledge and Predictions

A prediction is a guess about what will happen next. Readers are constantly making predictions based on what they have read and what they already know. Making predictions is an important part of being an active reader. Consider the following sentence: *Staring at the computer screen in shock, Kim blindly reached over for the brimming glass of water on the shelf to her side.* The sentence suggests that Kim is agitated and that she is not looking at the glass she is going to pick up, so a reader might predict that she is going to knock the glass over. Of course, not every prediction will be accurate: perhaps Kim will pick the glass up cleanly. Nevertheless, the author has certainly created the expectation that the water might be spilled. Predictions are always subject to revision as the reader acquires more information.

Problem-Solution Text Structure

Some nonfiction texts are organized to present a problem followed by a solution. In this type of text, it is common for the problem to be explained before the solution is offered. In some cases, as when the problem is well known, the solution may be briefly introduced at the beginning. Other times, the entire passage will focus on the solution, and the problem will be referenced only occasionally. This is common when the author can assume that the reading audience is already familiar with the problem. Some texts will outline multiple solutions to a problem, leaving the reader to choose among them. If the author has an interest or an allegiance to one solution, he may fail to mention or may describe inaccurately some of the other solutions. Readers should be careful of the author's agenda when reading a problem-solution text. Only by understanding the author's point of view and interests can one develop a proper judgment of the proposed solution.

Descriptive Text

In a sense, almost all writing is descriptive, insofar as it seeks to describe events, ideas, or people to the reader. Some texts, however, are primarily concerned with description. A descriptive text focuses on a particular subject, and attempts to depict it in a way that will be clear to the reader. Descriptive texts contain many adjectives and adverbs, words that give shades of meaning and create a more detailed mental picture for the reader. A descriptive text fails when it is unclear or vague to the reader. On the other hand, however, a descriptive text that compiles too much detail can be boring and overwhelming to the reader. A descriptive text will certainly be informative, and it may be persuasive and entertaining as well. Descriptive writing is a challenge for the author, but when it is done well, it can be fun to read.

Comparing and Contrasting

When an author describes the ways in which two things are alike, he or she is comparing them. When the author describes the ways in which two things are different, he or she is contrasting them. The "compare and contrast" essay is one of the most common forms in nonfiction. It is often signaled with certain words: a comparison may be indicated with such words as *both*, *same*, *like*, *too*, and *as well*; while a contrast may be indicated by words like *but*, *however*, *on the other hand*, *instead*, and *yet*. Of course, comparisons and contrasts may be implicit without using any such signaling language. A single sentence may both compare and contrast. Consider the sentence *Brian and Sheila love ice cream, but Brian prefers vanilla and Sheila prefers strawberry*. In one sentence, the author has described both a similarity (love of ice cream) and a difference (favorite flavor).

CAUSE AND EFFECT

One of the most common text structures is cause and effect. A cause is an act or event that makes something happen, and an effect is the thing that happens as a result of that cause. A cause-and-effect relationship is not always explicit, but there are some words in English that signal causality. These words include *since*, *because*, and *as a result*. As an example, consider the sentence *Because the sky was clear, Ron did not bring an umbrella*. The cause is the clear sky, and the effect is that Ron did not bring an umbrella. Sometimes the cause-and-effect relationship will not be clearly noted. For instance, the sentence *He was late and missed the meeting* does not contain any signaling words, but it still contains a cause (he was late) and an effect (he missed the meeting). It is possible for a single cause to have multiple effects, or for a single effect to have multiple causes. Also, an effect can in turn be the cause of another effect in what is known as a cause-and-effect chain.

AUTHOR'S POSITION

In order to be an effective reader, one must pay attention to the author's position and purpose. Even those texts that seem objective and impartial, like textbooks, have some sort of position and bias. Readers need to take these positions into account when considering the author's message. When an author uses emotional language or clearly favors one side of an argument, his position is clear. However, the author's position may be evident not only in what he writes, but in what he doesn't write. For this reason, it is sometimes necessary to review some other texts on the same topic in order to develop a view of the author's position. If this is not possible, then it may be useful to acquire a little background personal information about the author. When the only source of information is the text, however, the reader should look for language and argumentation that seems to indicate a particular stance on the subject.

AUTHOR'S PURPOSE

An author's purpose is often evident in the organization of the text. For instance, if the text has headings and subheadings, if key terms are in bold, and if the author makes his main idea clear from the beginning, then the likely purpose of the text is to inform. If the author begins by making a claim and then makes various arguments to support that claim, the purpose is probably to persuade. If the author is telling a story, or is more interested in holding the attention of the reader than in making a particular point or delivering information, then his purpose is most likely to entertain. As a reader, it is best to judge an author on how well he accomplishes his purpose. In other words, it is not entirely fair to complain that a textbook is boring: if the text is clear and easy to understand, then the author has done his job. Similarly, a storyteller should not be judged too harshly for getting some facts wrong, so long as he is able to give pleasure to the reader.

NARRATIVE PASSAGE

A narrative passage is a story. Narratives can be either fiction or nonfiction, but there are a few elements that a text must have in order to be classified as a narrative. To begin with, the text must have a plot. That is, it must describe a series of events. If it is a good narrative, these events will be interesting and emotionally engaging to the reader. A narrative also has characters. These could be people, animals, or even inanimate objects, so long as they participate in the plot. A narrative passage often contains figurative language, which is meant to stimulate the imagination of the reader by making comparisons and observations. A metaphor, which is a description of one thing in terms of another, is a common piece of figurative language. *The moon was a frosty snowball* is an example of a metaphor: it is untrue in the literal sense, but it suggests a certain mood for the reader. Narratives often proceed in a clear sequence, but they do not need to do so.

Expository Passage

An expository passage aims to inform and enlighten the reader. It is nonfiction and usually centers around a simple, easily defined topic. Since the goal of exposition is to teach, such a passage should be as clear as possible. It is common for an expository passage to contain helpful organizing words, like *first, next, for example,* and *therefore*. These words keep the reader oriented in the text. Although expository passages do not need to feature colorful language and artful writing, they are often more effective when they do. For a reader, the challenge of expository passages is to maintain steady attention. Expository passages are not always about subjects in which a reader will naturally be interested, and the writer is often more concerned with clarity and comprehensibility than with engaging the reader. For this reason, expository passages can be dull. Making notes is a good way to maintain focus when reading an expository passage.

Technical Passage

A technical passage is written to describe a complex object or process. Technical writing is common in medical and technological fields, in which complicated mathematical, scientific, and engineering ideas need to be explained simply and clearly. To ease comprehension, a technical passage usually proceeds in a very logical order. Technical passages often have clear headings and subheadings which are used to keep the reader oriented in the text. It is also common for these passages to break sections up with numbers or letters. Many technical passages look more like an outline than a piece of prose. The amount of difficult vocabulary or field-specific jargon will vary depending on the intended audience. As much as possible, technical passages try to avoid language that the reader will have to research in order to understand the message, though this is not always possible

Persuasive Passage

A persuasive passage is meant to change the reader's mind or lead her into agreement with the author. The persuasive intent may be obvious or it may be quite difficult to discern. In some cases, a persuasive passage will be indistinguishable from an informative passage: it will make an assertion and offer supporting details. However, a persuasive passage is more likely to make claims based on opinion and to appeal to the reader's emotions. Persuasive passages may not describe alternate positions and, when they do, they often display significant bias. It may be clear that a persuasive passage is giving the author's viewpoint or the passage may adopt a seemingly objective tone. A persuasive passage is successful if it can make a convincing argument and win the trust of the reader.

Historical Context

Historical context has a profound influence on literature: the events, knowledge base, and assumptions of an author's time color every aspect of his or her work. Sometimes, authors hold opinions and use language that would be considered inappropriate or immoral in a modern setting but that was acceptable in the author's time. As a reader, one should consider how the historical context influenced a work and also how today's opinions and ideas shape the way modern readers read the works of the past. For instance, in most societies of the past, women were treated as second-class citizens. An author who wrote in 18th-century England might sound sexist to modern readers, even if that author was relatively feminist in his time. Readers should not have to excuse the faulty assumptions and prejudices of the past, but they should appreciate that a person's thoughts and words are, in part, a result of the time and culture in which they live or lived, and it is perhaps unfair to expect writers to avoid all of the errors of their times.

LITERATURE FROM DIFFERENT CULTURES PRESENTS SIMILAR THEMES

Even a brief study of world literature suggests that writers from vastly different cultures address similar themes. For instance, works like the *Odyssey* and *Hamlet* both tackle the individual's battle for self-control and independence. In every culture, authors address themes of personal growth and the struggle for maturity. Another universal theme is the conflict between the individual and society. In works as culturally disparate as *Native Son*, the *Aeneid*, and *1984*, authors dramatize how people struggle to maintain their personalities and dignity in large, sometimes oppressive groups. Many cultures also have versions of the hero's (or heroine's) journey, in which an adventurous person must overcome many obstacles in order to gain greater knowledge, power, and perspective. Some famous works that treat this theme are the *Epic of Gilgamesh*, Dante's *Divine Comedy*, and *Don Quixote.*

DRAWING CONCLUSIONS

When asked for a *conclusion* that may be drawn, look for critical "hedge" phrases, such as likely, may, can, will often, sometimes, etc, often, almost, mostly, usually, generally, rarely, sometimes.

Test writers insert these hedge phrases to cover every possibility. An answer can be wrong simply because it leaves no room for exception. Extreme positive or negative answers (such as always, never, etc.) are usually not correct.

ANSWERING QUESTIONS ONLY FROM THE READING

When testing, the reader should not use any outside knowledge that is not gathered from the reading passage to answer the related questions unless specifically instructed to do so. Correct answers can be derived straight from the reading passage.

FIGURE OF SPEECH

A figure of speech, sometimes termed a rhetorical figure or device, is a word or phrase that departs from straightforward, literal language. Figures of speech are often used and crafted for emphasis, freshness of expression, or clarity. However, clarity may suffer from their use.

As an example of the figurative use of a word, consider the following sentence: I am going to crown you.

It may mean:

- I am going to place a literal crown on your head.
- I am going to symbolically exalt you to the place of kingship.
- I am going to punch you in the head with my clenched fist.
- I am going to put a second checker on top of your checker to signify that it has become a king.

LITERARY GENRES

Literary genres refer to the basic generic types of poetry, drama, fiction, and nonfiction. It is a method of classifying and analyzing literature. There are numerous subdivisions within each genre. Fiction, for instance, includes such subcategories as novels, novellas, and short stories. Drama may also be subdivided into comedy, tragedy, and many other categories. Poetry and nonfiction have their own distinct divisions.

Genres can overlap and the distinctions among them are sometimes blurred, such as that between the nonfiction novel and docudrama. However, the use of genres is helpful to the reader as a setting that guides our responses to a work. The genre sets expectations and forms the framework within which we read and evaluate a work. This framework will guide both our understanding and interpretation of the work. It is a useful tool for both literary criticism and analysis.

Fiction

Fiction is a general term for any form of literary narrative that is invented or imagined rather than factual. For those individuals who equate fact with truth, the imagined or invented character of fiction tends to render it relatively unimportant or trivial among the genres. Defenders of fiction are quick to point out that the fictional mode is an essential part of being. The ability to imagine or discuss what-if plots, characters, and events is clearly part of the human experience.

Fiction is much wider than simply prose fiction. Songs, ballads, epics, and narrative poems are also examples of fiction. A full definition of fiction must include not only the work itself but also the framework in which it is read. Literary fiction can also be defined as not true rather than nonexistent, as many works of historical fiction refer to real people, places, and events that are treated imaginatively as if they were true. These imaginary elements enrich and broaden literary expression.

Prose

Prose is derived from the Latin and means "straightforward discourse." Prose fiction, although having many categories, may be divided into three main groups:

1. Short stories: a fictional narrative; the length varies but is usually under 20,000 words. Short stories usually have only a few characters and generally describe one major event or insight. The short story as we know it began in magazines in the late 1800s and has flourished ever since.
2. Novels: a longer work of fiction, often containing a large cast of characters and extensive plotting. The emphasis may be on an event, action, social problems, or any experience. Novels may also be written in verse.
3. Novellas: a work of narrative fiction longer than a short story but shorter than a novel. Novellas may also be called short novels or novelettes. They originated from the German tradition and have become common forms in all of the world's literature.

Prose Fiction

A character is a person intimately involved with the plot and development of the novel. There is usually a physical description of the character, but this is often omitted in modern and postmodern novels. These works may focus on the psychological state or motivation of the character. The choice of a character's name may give valuable clues to his role in the work.

Characters are said to be flat or round. Flat characters tend to be minor figures in the story, changing little or not at all. Round characters (those understood from a well-rounded view) are more central to the story and tend to change as the plot unfolds. Stock characters are similar to flat characters, filling out the story without influencing it.

Modern literature has been greatly affected by Freudian psychology, giving rise to such devices as the interior monologue and magical realism as methods of understanding characters in a work. These give the reader a more complex understanding of the inner lives of the characters and enrich the understanding of relationships between characters.

Many elements influence a work of prose fiction. Some important ones are:

1. Speech and dialogue: Characters may speak for themselves or through the narrator. Dialogue may be realistic or fantastic, depending on the author's aim.
2. Thoughts and mental processes: There may be internal dialogue used as a device for plot development or character understanding.
3. Dramatic involvement: Some narrators encourage readers to become involved in the events of the story, whereas others attempt to distance readers through literary devices.
4. Action: This is any information that advances the plot or involves new interactions between the characters.
5. Duration: The time frame of the work may be long or short, and the relationship between described time and narrative time may vary.
6. Setting and description: Is the setting critical to the plot or characters? How are the action scenes described?
7. Themes: This is any point of view or topic given sustained attention.
8. Symbolism: Authors often veil meanings through imagery and other literary constructions.

Novel

The following are important questions to address to better understand the voice and role of the narrator and incorporate that voice into an overall understanding of the novel:

- Who is the narrator of the novel? What is the narrator's perspective, first person or third person? What is the role of the narrator in the plot? Are there changes in narrators or the perspective of narrators?
- Does the narrator explain things in the novel, or does meaning emerge from the plot and events? The personality of the narrator is important. He may have a vested interest in a character or event described. Some narratives follow the time sequence of the plot, whereas others do not. A narrator may express approval or disapproval about a character or events in the work.
- Tone is an important aspect of the narration. Who is actually being addressed by the narrator? Is the tone familiar or formal, intimate or impersonal? Does the vocabulary suggest clues about the narrator?

Reading Novels Slowly and with a Critical Eye

Reading novels and novellas offer a different experience than short stories. Our imagination is more active as we review what we have read, imagine ourselves as characters in the novel, and try to guess what will happen next. Suspense, surprise, fantasy, fear, anxiety, compassion, and a host of other emotions and feelings may be stirred by a provocative novel. Reading these longer works of fiction is a cumulative process. Some elements of a novel have a great impact, while others may go virtually unnoticed. Therefore, as novels are read with a critical eye to language, it is helpful to perceive and identify larger patterns and movements in the work as a whole. This will benefit the reader by placing characters and events in perspective, and will enrich the reading experience greatly. Novels should be savored rather than gulped. Careful reading and thoughtful analysis of the major themes of the novel are essential to a clear understanding of the work.

Speech and Dialogue in Drama

Analysis of speech and dialogue is important in the critical study of drama. Some playwrights use speech to develop their characters. Speeches may be long or short, and are written in as normal prose or blank verse. Some characters have a unique way of speaking which illuminates aspects of the drama, which makes emphasis and tone important. Does the author make clear the tone in which lines are to be spoken, or is this open to interpretation? Sometimes there are various possibilities in tone with regard to delivering lines.

Asides and soliloquies can be important in plot and character development. Asides are short comment or sentence directed to the audience; the other characters are not privy to the lines. This may be a method of advancing or explaining the plot in a subtle manner. Soliloquies are similar, but are longer speeches that will contain more dramatic expression of feelings and emotions. They are opportunities for character development, plot enhancement, and to give insight to characters motives. Careful study of these elements provides a reader with an abundance of clues to the major themes and plot of the work.

Reading Drama

A play is written to be spoken aloud. The drama is in many ways inseparable from performance. Reading drama ideally involves using imagination to visualize and re-create the play with characters and settings. The reader stages the play in his imagination, watching characters interact and developments unfold. Sometimes this involves simulating a theatrical presentation; other times it involves imagining the events. In either case, the reader is imagining the unwritten to re-create the dramatic experience. Novels present some of the same problems, but a narrator will provide much more information about the setting, characters, inner dialogues, and many other supporting details. In drama, much of this is missing, and we are required to use our powers of projection and imagination to taste the full flavor of the dramatic work. There are many empty spaces in dramatic texts that must be filled by the reader to fully appreciate the work.

An oft-heard criticism of reading drama is that the experience pales when compared to watching a performance. There are, however, some advantages to reading drama as text:

1. Freedom of point of view and perspective: Text is free of interpretations of actors, directors, producers, and technical staging.
2. Additional information: The text of a drama may be accompanied by notes or prefaces placing the work in a social or historical context. Stage directions may also provide relevant information about the author's purpose. None of this is typically available at live or filmed performances.
3. Study and understanding: Difficult or obscure passages may be studied at leisure and supplemented by explanatory works. This is particularly true of older plays with unfamiliar language, which cannot be fully understood without an opportunity to study the material.

Reading Dramatic Dialogue

Dramatic dialogue can be difficult to interpret, and it changes depending upon the tone used and which words are emphasized. Where the stresses, or meters, of dramatic dialogue fall can determine meaning. Tone is also important, and it expresses a range of possible emotions and feelings that cannot be readily discerned from the script of a play. The reader must add tone to the words to understand the full meaning of a passage. Recognizing tone is a cumulative process as the reader begins to understand the characters and situations in the play. Other elements that influence the interpretation of dialogue include the setting, possible reactions of the characters to the speech, and imagined gestures or facial expressions of the character. There are no firm rules to guide the interpretation of dramatic speech. An open and flexible attitude is essential in interpreting dramatic dialogue.

DIALECT, DIALECT MIXTURES, DIALECT GEOGRAPHY, DIALECT ATLAS, AND DIALECT CONTINUUM

Dialect is any distinct variety of a language, especially one spoken in a region or part of a country. The criterion for distinguishing dialects from languages is that of *mutual understanding*. For example, people who speak Dutch cannot understand English unless they have learned it. But a speaker from Amsterdam can understand one from Antwerp; therefore, they speak different dialects of the same language. This is, however, a matter of degree; there are languages in which different dialects are unintelligible.

Dialect mixtures are the presence of elements from neighboring dialects in the speaker's own dialect. The study of speech differences from one geographical area to another is called dialect geography. A dialect atlas is a map showing distribution of dialects in a given area. A dialect continuum shows a progressive shift in dialects across a territory, such that adjacent dialects are understandable, but those at the extremes are not.

PLOT LINE

Every plot line follows the same stages. One can identify each of these stages in every story they read. These stages are: the introduction, rising action, conflict, climax, falling action, and resolution. The introduction tells the reader what the story will be about and sets up the plot. The rising action is what happens that leads up to the conflict, which is some sort of problem that arises, with the climax at its peak. The falling action is what happens after the climax of the conflict. The resolution is the conclusion and often has the final solution to the problem in the conflict. A plot line looks like this:

The author will always have a point of view about a story before they draw up a plot line. The author will know what events they want to take place, how they want the characters to interact, and how the story will resolve. An author will also have an opinion on the topic, or series of events, which is presented in the story, based on their own prior experience and beliefs.

A story can be taken in whatever direction the author wishes. A story will often make sense based on societal norms, but the author can purposely choose to go against these norms to shock the reader. For example, if an author wrote a story about a man who enjoyed living in the bayous of Louisiana, the audience would not expect the character to promptly move to Alaska. Sometimes an author will put a twist in a story just to surprise the reader.

STAGE DIRECTIONS

Action is a crucial element in the production of a dramatic work. Many dramas contain little dialogue and much action. In these cases, it is essential for the reader to carefully study stage directions and visualize the action on the stage. Benefits of understanding stage directions include knowing which characters are on the stage at all times, who is speaking to whom, and following these patterns through changes of scene.

Stage directions also provide additional information, some of which is not available to a live audience. The nature of the physical space where the action occurs is vital, and stage directions help with this. The historical context of the period is important in understanding what the playwright was working with in terms of theaters and physical space. The type of staging possible for the author is a good guide to the spatial elements of a production.

Analogy

An analogy is a comparison of two things. The words in the analogy are connected by a certain (sometimes undetermined) relationship. Look at this analogy: moo is to cow as quack is to duck. This analogy compares the sound that a cow makes with the sound that a duck makes. Even if the word 'quack' was not given, one could figure out it is the correct word to complete the analogy based on the relationship between the words 'moo' and 'cow'. Some common relationships for analogies include synonyms, antonyms, part to whole, definition, and actor to action.

Paraphrasing and Summarizing

Paraphrasing and summarizing are two methods one can use to help them understand what they read. When paraphrasing, one puts what they have read into their own words, rephrasing what the author has written to make it their own, to "translate" all of what the author says to their own words, including as many details as they can. When summarizing, on the other hand, one does not include many details, but rather simply the main idea of the text. Often times, a summary can be done in just one or two sentences, boiling down the author's words into just main idea.

Structural Analysis

The term *structural analysis* refers to looking at the parts of a word and breaking it down into its different components to determine the word's meaning. The parts of a word include the prefix, suffix, and the root word. By looking at the root of an unfamiliar word, the reader can get a basic sense of what the word means. For example, the word *joy* means "great happiness" and the suffix -*ful* means "full of". If the reader did not know what the word *joyful* meant, he or she could break the word down into these components to figure out its meaning. The word *joyful*, when looked at in pieces, means "full of happiness". By knowing a multitude of meanings for root words, prefixes, and suffixes, a reader can better understand difficult passages of text.

Organizing Ideas from a Text

Two of the most common ways to organize ideas from a text include paraphrasing and summarizing. Paraphrasing involves taking another's ideas and putting them into one's own words. A paraphrase can involve a single paragraph or encompass the entire main idea of a selection. A summary is used to write the main idea and supporting points of a story in a succinct manner. Summaries are useful when describing the specific points that need to be remembered from an entire story.

Ideas from a text can also be organized using graphic organizers. A spider-map takes a main idea from the story and places it in a bubble, with supporting points branching off the main idea. An outline can be useful for diagramming the main and supporting points of the entire story. A Venn diagram is useful for classifying information as separate or overlapping, whereas a timeline can chronicle the order of events in a story.

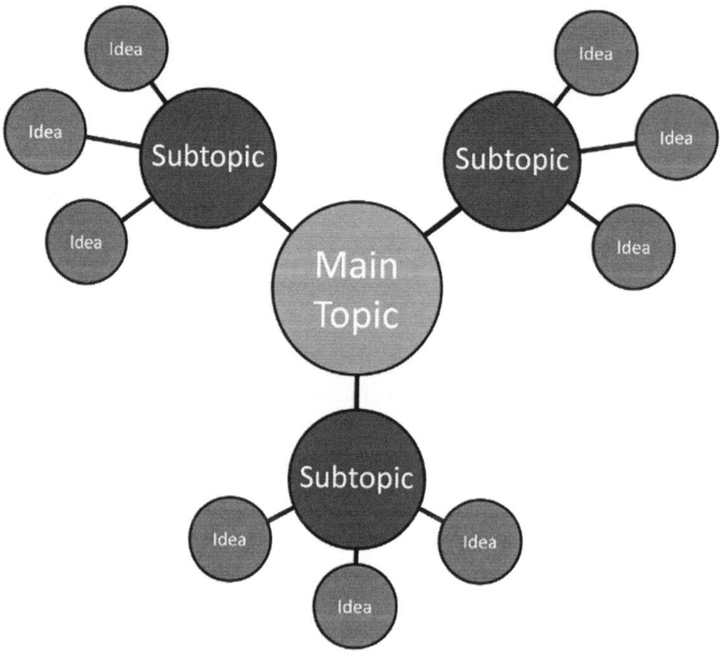

Defending Response or Interpretation

Readers can interpret text and respond to it in a number of ways. Using textual support helps defend your response or interpretation because it roots your thinking in the text. You are interpreting based on information in the text and not simply your own ideas. When crafting a response, look for important quotes and details from the text to help bolster your argument. If you are writing about a character's personality trait, for example, use details from the text to show that the character acted in such a way. You can also include statistics and facts from a nonfiction text to strengthen your response. For example, instead of writing, "A lot of people use cell phones," use statistics to provide the exact number. This strengthens your argument because it is more precise.

Figurative Language

Figurative language is language that goes beyond the literal meaning of the words. Descriptive language that evokes imagery in the reader's mind is one type of figurative language. Exaggeration is also one type of figurative language. Also, when you compare two things, you are using figurative language. Similes and metaphors are ways of comparing things, and both are types of figurative language commonly found in poetry. An example of figurative language (a simile in this case) is: *The child howled like a coyote when her mother told her to pick up the toys.* In this example, the child's howling is compared to that of a coyote. Figurative language is descriptive in nature and helps the reader understand the sound being made in this sentence.

Author's Motivations

A text is **credible**, or believable, when the author is both knowledgeable and objective. When evaluating the credibility of a text, it is important to look at the author of the text. The author's motive should be the dissemination of information. When an author writes a persuasive text, his motive is to persuade the reader to do or believe something. If a text is being written by an author with a specific agenda (e.g., a business owner seeking more profit), that text is going to be biased in a particular direction. The author's motivations for writing the text play a critical role in determining the credibility of the text and must be evaluated when assessing that credibility.

Determining the Contextual Meaning of a Word with Multiple Definitions

When a word has more than one meaning, it can be tricky to determine how it is being used in a given sentence. Consider the verb *cleave*, which bizarrely can mean either "join" or "separate." When a reader comes upon this word, she will have to select the definition that makes the most sense. So, take as an example the following sentence: "The birds cleaved together as they flew from the oak tree." Immediately, the presence of the word *together* should suggest that in this sentence *cleave* is being used to mean *"join."* In contrast, the sentence, "Hermione's knife cleaved the bread cleanly." would have a different result. It doesn't make sense for a knife to join bread together, so the word must be meant to indicate separation. Discovering the meaning of a word with multiple meanings requires the same tricks as defining an unknown word: looking for contextual clues and evaluating substituted words.

Prefixes and Suffixes to Identify Unfamiliar Words

Sometimes, a text will contain an unfamiliar word that cannot be defined from context. It may be possible to obtain some information from the word's structure. Specifically, the word may have a common prefix or suffix that will provide some clues about meaning. Prefixes are common letter combinations at the beginning of words, while suffixes are common letter combinations at the end. The main part of the word is known as the root. Some of the most common prefixes are *ex-*, *in-*, *de-*, and *anti-*. These prefixes mean "out of," "not," "down," and "against," as in *exile*, *inconceivable*, *descend*, and *antipathy*. Some of the most common suffixes are *–ism*, *-tion*, and *–ology*. These suffixes mean "belief system," "action of," and "science of," as in *communism*, *locomotion*, and *biology*. It is important to recognize the common prefixes and suffixes, as this knowledge can illuminate at least part of the meaning of an unfamiliar word.

Metaphors

A metaphor is a type of figurative language in which the writer equates one thing with a different thing. For instance, in the sentence "The bird was an arrow arcing through the sky," the arrow is serving as a metaphor for the bird. The point of a metaphor is to encourage the reader to think about the thing being described in a different way. Using this example, we are being asked to envision the bird's flight as being similar to the arc of an arrow, so we will imagine it to be swift, bending, etc. Metaphors are a way for the author to describe without being direct and obvious. Metaphors are a more lyrical and suggestive way of providing information. Note that the thing to which a metaphor refers will not always be mentioned explicitly by the author. For instance, consider the following description of a forest in winter: "Swaying skeletons reached for the sky and groaned as the wind blew through them." The author is clearly using *skeletons* as a metaphor for leafless trees. This metaphor creates a spooky tone while inspiring the reader's imagination.

Hyperbole

Hyperbole is overstatement for effect. The following sentence is an example of hyperbole: *He jumped ten feet in the air when he heard the good news.* Obviously, no person has the ability to jump ten feet in the air. The author hyperbolizes not because he believes the statement will be taken literally, but because the exaggeration conveys the extremity of emotion. Consider how much less colorful the sentence would be if the author simply said, "He jumped when he heard the good news." Hyperbole can be dangerous if the author does not exaggerate enough. For instance, if the author wrote, "He jumped two feet in the air when he heard the good news," the reader might not be sure whether this is actually true or just hyperbole. Of course, in many situations this distinction will not really matter. However, an author should avoid confusing or vague hyperbole when he needs to maintain credibility or authority with readers.

Antonyms

Antonyms are opposites. *Light* and *dark*, *up* and *down*, *right* and *left*, *good* and *bad*: these are all sets of antonyms. It is important to distinguish between antonyms and pairs of words that are simply different. *Black* and *gray*, for instance, are not antonyms because gray is not the opposite of black. *Black* and *white*, on the other hand, are antonyms. Not every word has an antonym. For instance, many nouns do not. What would be the antonym of *chair*, after all? On a standardized test, the questions related to antonyms are more likely to concern adjectives. Remember that adjectives are words that describe a noun. Some common adjectives include *red*, *fast*, *skinny*, and *sweet*. Of these four examples, only *red* lacks a group of obvious antonyms.

Similes

A simile is a figurative expression similar to a metaphor, though it requires the use of a distancing word like *like* or *as*. Some examples are "The sun was like an orange," "eager as a beaver," and "nimble as a mountain goat." Because a simile includes *like* or *as*, it creates a little space between the description and the thing being described. If an author says that a house was "like a shoebox," the tone is slightly different than if the author said that the house *was* a shoebox. In a simile, the author indicates an awareness that the description is not the same thing as the thing being described. In a metaphor, there is no such distinction, even though one may safely assume that the author is aware of it. This is a subtle difference, but authors will alternately use metaphors and similes depending on their intended tone.

Personification

Personification is the description of the nonhuman as if it were human. Literally, the word means the process of making something into a person. There is a wide range of approaches to personification, from common expressions like "whispering wind" to full novels like *Animal Farm*, by George Orwell, in which the Bolshevik Revolution is reenacted by farmyard animals. The general intent of personification is to describe things in a manner that will be comprehensible to readers. When an author states that a tree "groans" in the wind, she of course does not mean that the tree is emitting a low, pained sound from its mouth. Instead, she means that the tree is making a noise similar to a human groan. Of course, this personification establishes a tone of sadness or suffering. A different tone would be established if the author said the tree was "swaying" or "dancing."

Alliteration and Assonance

Alliteration is the repetition of initial sounds in a series of words. An example of alliteration could be "thundering through the thickets," in which the initial *th* sound is used in four consecutive words. Alliteration draws attention to itself, which may be a good or a bad thing. Authors should be conscious of the character of the sound to be repeated. In the above example, a *th* sound is somewhat difficult to make quickly in four consecutive words, so the phrase conveys a little of the difficulty of moving through tall grass. If the author is indeed trying to suggest this difficulty, then the alliteration is a success. Consider, however, the description of eyes as "glassy globes of glitter." This is definitely alliteration, since the initial *gl* sound is used three times. However, one might question whether this awkward sound is appropriate for a description of pretty eyes. The phrase is not especially pleasant to the ear, and therefore is probably not effective as alliteration. Assonance is the repetition of vowel sounds in a phrase, as in "Low and slow, he rolled the coal." Assonance functions in much the same way as alliteration.

Irony

Irony is a statement that suggests its opposite. In other words, it is when an author or character says one thing but means another. For example, imagine a man walks in his front door, covered in mud and in tattered clothes. His wife asks him, "How was your day?" and he says "Great!" The man's comment is an example of irony. As in this example, irony often depends on information the reader obtains elsewhere. There is a fine distinction between irony and sarcasm. Irony is any statement in which the literal meaning is opposite from the intended meaning, while sarcasm is a statement of this type that is also insulting to the person at whom it is directed. A sarcastic statement suggests that the other person is stupid enough to believe an obviously false statement is true. Irony is a bit more subtle than sarcasm.

Understatement

Understatement is the opposite of hyperbole. This device discounts or downplays something. Think about someone who climbs Mount Everest. Then, they say that the journey was *a little stroll.* As with other types of figurative language, understatement has a range of uses. The device may show self-defeat or modesty as in the Mount Everest example. However, some may think of understatement as false modesty (i.e., an attempt to bring attention to you or a situation). For example, a woman is praised on her diamond engagement ring. The woman says, *Oh, this little thing?* Her understatement might be heard as stuck-up or unfeeling.

Review Video: Hyperbole and Understatement
Visit mometrix.com/academy and enter code: 308470

Metonymy and Synecdoche

Metonymy is referring to one thing in terms of another, closely related thing. This is similar to metaphor, but there is less distance between the description and the thing being described. An example of metonymy is referring to the news media as the "press," when of course the press is only the device by which newspapers are printed. Metonymy is a way of referring to something without having to repeat its name constantly. Synecdoche, on the other hand, is referring to a whole by one of its parts. An example of synecdoche would be calling a police officer a "badge." Synecdoche, like metonymy, is a handy way of referring without having to overuse certain words. It also allows the writer to emphasize aspects of the thing being described. For instance, referring to businessmen as "suits" suggests professionalism, conformity, and drabness.

Essays

Essays are generally defined to describe a prose composition, are relatively brief (rarely exceeding 25 pages), and deal with a specific topic. Originally, essays tended to be informal in tone and exploratory and tentative in approach and conclusions. In more modern writing, essays have been divided into the formal and informal. The formal essays have dominated the professional and scientific fields, whereas the informal style is written primarily to entertain or give opinions. Writers should be mindful of the style of essay their subject lends itself to and conform to the conventions of that style.

Some types of essays, particularly scientific and academic writing, have style manuals to guide the format and conventions of the writing. The Modern Language Association and the American Psychological Association have two of the most widely followed style manuals. They are widely available for writers' reference.

Preparation Involved in Writing

Effective writing requires preparation. The planning process includes everything done prior to drafting. Depending on the project, this could take a few minutes or several months. Elements in planning include considering the purpose of the writing, exploring a topic, developing a working thesis, gathering necessary materials, and devising a plan for organizing the writing. The organizational plan may vary in length and components, from a detailed outline to a stack of research cards. The organizational plan is a guide to help draft a writing project. The plan may change as writing progresses, but having such a guide is essential to keeping a project on track. Planning is usually an ongoing process throughout the writing, but it is essential to begin with a structure.

Purposes of Writing

What is the main purpose of the proposed piece? This may be very clear and focused, or it may be ambiguous. A writer should be clear about the purpose of his or her writing, as this will determine the direction and elements of the work. Generally, purposes may be divided into three groups:

1. To entertain
2. To persuade or convince
3. To educate or inform

Some or all of these purposes may be the goal in a given writing assignment. It is helpful to try to identify the major purpose of a writing piece, as well as any secondary purposes involved. Purpose in writing must be linked closely to the writer's goals in undertaking the assignment. In academic settings, it is usually more accurate to think in terms of several goals. A student may wish to convince the audience in an entertaining and informative fashion. However, one goal should be paramount: Expectations of the instructor play an important role in an academic assignment.

Examples and Illustrations

Examples are a common method of development and may be effectively used when a reader may ask, "For example?" Examples are selected instances, not an inclusive catalog. They may be used to suggest the validity of topic sentences.

Illustrations are extended examples, sometimes presented in story form for interest. They usually require several sentences each, so they are used sparingly. Well-selected illustrations can be a colorful and vivid way of developing a point. Stories that command reader interest, developed in a story form, can be powerful methods of emphasizing key points in an essay. Stories and illustrations should be specific and relate directly to a point or points being made in the text. They allow more colorful language and instill a sense of human interest in a subject. Used judiciously, illustrations and stories are excellent devices.

Analogies and Cause and Effect

Analogies draw comparisons between items that appear to have nothing in common. Analogies are employed by writers to attempt to provoke fresh thoughts and changed feelings about a subject. They may be used to make the unfamiliar more familiar, to clarify an abstract point, or to argue a point. Although analogies are effective literary devices, they should be used thoughtfully in arguments. Two things may be alike in some respects but completely different in others.

Cause and effect is an excellent device best used when the cause and effect are generally accepted as true. As a matter of argument, cause and effect is usually too complex and subject to other interpretations to be used successfully. A valid way of using cause and effect is to state the effect in the topic sentence of a paragraph and add the causes in the body of the paragraph. This adds logic and form to a paragraph and usually makes it more effective.

FALLACIOUS ARGUMENTS

A number of unreasonable argumentative tactics are known as logical fallacies. Most fallacies are misguided uses of legitimate argumentative arguments.

Generalizing is drawing a conclusion from an array of facts using inductive reasoning. These conclusions are a probability, not a certainty. The fallacy known as a hasty generalization is a conclusion based on insufficient or unrepresentative evidence. Stereotyping is a hasty generalization about a group. This is common because of the human tendency to perceive selectively. Many observations are made through a filter of preconceptions, prejudices, and attitudes.

Analogies point out similarities between disparate things. When an analogy is unreasonable, it is called a false analogy. This usually consists of assuming if two things are alike in one respect, they must be alike in others. This, of course, may or may not be true. Each comparison must be independently verified to make the argument valid.

TONE AND MOOD

Tone and mood in writing refer to the attitude the author displays toward the subject. Although tone is usually associated with attitude, it may not be identified with the writer. If the language is ambiguous, tone becomes very difficult to ascertain. A common tone in contemporary writing is irony. Tone is communicated by the writer's choice of language.

Tone is distinguished from mood, which is the feeling the writing evokes. Tone and mood may often be similar, but they also can be significantly different. Mood often depends on the manner in which words and language are employed by the writer. In a sense, tone and mood are two sides of a coin that color language and enliven the total approach of a writer to the subject. Mood and tone add richness and texture to words, bringing them alive in a deliberate strategy by the writer.

POINT OF VIEW

Point of view is the **perspective** from which writing occurs. There are several possibilities:

- *First person* is written so that the *I* of the story is a participant or observer.
- *Second person* is written directly to the reader. It is a device to draw the reader in more closely. In second person, "you" the reader, are the one taking action in a sentence.
- *Third person*, the most traditional form of point of view, is the omniscient narrator, in which the narrative voice, presumed to be the writer's, is presumed to know everything about the characters, plot, and action. Most novels use this point of view.

1. A *multiple point of view* is narration delivered from the perspective of several characters.

In modern writing, the stream-of-consciousness technique is often used. Developed fully by James Joyce, this technique uses an interior monologue that provides the narration through the thoughts, impressions, and fantasies of the narrator.

RECURSIVE NATURE OF THE WRITING PROCESS

The process of writing is described as recursive. This means that the goals and parts of the writing process are often a seamless flow, constantly influencing each other without clear boundaries. The steps in the writing process occur organically, with planning, drafting, and revising all taking place simultaneously, in no necessary or orderly fashion. The writer rarely pays attention to the recursive patterns. The process unfolds naturally, without attention or dependence on a predetermined sequence. The writing process is a series of recursive activities, which rarely occur in a linear fashion, rather moving back and forth between planning, drafting, revising, more planning, more drafting, polishing until the writing is complete. Forthcoming topics will cover many parts of the process individually, but they go on together as a seamless flow.

Conventions in Writing

Conventions in writing are traditional assumptions or practices used by authors of all types of text. Some basic conventions have survived through the centuries, for example, the assumption that a first-person narrator in a work is telling the truth. Others, such as having characters in melodramas speak in asides to the audience, have become outmoded. Conventions are particularly important in specialized types of writing that demand specific formats and styles. This is true of scientific and research papers, as well as much of academic and business writing. This formality has relaxed somewhat in several areas but still holds true for many fields of technical writing. Conventions are particularly useful for writers working in various types of nonfiction writing, in which guidelines help the writer conform to the rules expected for that field. Conventions are part of the unspoken contract between writer and audience, and they should be respected.

Free Writing

Free writing is a form of brainstorming in a structured way. The method involves exploring a topic by writing about it for a certain period without stopping. A writer sets a time limit and begins writing in complete sentences everything that comes to mind about the topic. Writing continues without interruption until the set period expires. When time expires, read carefully everything that has been written down. Much of it may make little or no sense, but insights and observations may emerge that the free writer did not know existed in his or her mind. Writing has a unique quality of jogging loose ideas, and seeing a word or idea appear may trigger others. Free writing usually results in a fuller expression of ideas than brainstorming does because thoughts and associations are written more comprehensively. Both techniques can be used to complement one another and can yield much different results.

Reading Informational Texts

Thesaurus

A thesaurus is a tool that has synonyms of words. For example, if you look up the word *happy* in a thesaurus, you would see the words *content, pleased, glad, joyful*, and *delighted*. A thesaurus does not give a definition like a dictionary does, but you can use a thesaurus to help figure out the meaning of an unfamiliar word. If you are familiar with some of the synonyms of the word, you can determine a precise meaning of the unfamiliar word. For example, if you looked up the word *exultant* and saw the synonyms *overjoyed* and *thrilled,* this could lead you to its meaning "extremely happy."

Organizational Methods Used to Structure Text

Authors organize their writing based on the purpose of their text. Common organizational methods that authors use include: cause and effect, compare and contrast, inductive presentation of ideas, deductive presentation of ideas, and chronological order. Cause and effect is used to present the reasons that something happened. Compare and contrast is used to discuss the similarities and differences between two things. Inductive presentation of ideas starts with specific examples and moves to a general conclusion. Deductive presentation of ideas starts with a conclusion and then explains the examples used to arrive at the conclusion. Chronological order presents information in the order that it occurred.

Persuasive Technique of Logical Fallacies

The persuasive technique of logical fallacies is using common errors in reasoning to persuade someone of something. Two types of logical fallacies are slippery slope and hasty generalizations. In slippery slope, you say that if something happens it automatically means that something else will happen, even though this may not be true. An example of slippery slope would be to say that if a little shampoo gets your hair clean, a lot of shampoo would get it cleaner. This is not the case. Once your hair is clean, it cannot get any cleaner. Hasty generalization is drawing a conclusion too early. An example of a hasty generalization would be to say, "Even though I have only used this product for one day, I know it is going to change my life by saving me so much time."

Italics and Ellipses

Italics (words that are slanted to the right) are used to distinguish a particular word or phrase from the rest of the text. Italics are used for titles, vehicles, words of words, emphasis, and foreign words. Titles include those of books, magazines, movies, television shows, musical pieces, and artwork. Ellipses are three little dots in a row (...), used when omitting words in a quotation. Ellipses indicate that words are missing. The author needs to be careful, however, that the removal of words does not change the meaning of the quote. Ellipses are also used in more conversational writing, like e-mail, to indicate hesitation or faltering thoughts.

Explicit Information

Explicit information is information that is stated in a text. It is not something that is hinted at. A nonfiction text is usually made up of a main idea and supporting details. These supporting details are explicit: they are stated right in the text. They can be used to support an inference that is not stated in the text, or to support the main claims of an essay. Supporting information should be based on fact, not opinion. It should come from a reliable source and be something that others can verify. When trying to find textual evidence for what a text says explicitly, you will need to look for details that give more information about it.

Main idea and its relationship to supporting ideas

The main idea of a passage is what the passage is mostly about. It is the main point of the passage. Sometimes the main idea is stated in a passage by the use of a topic sentence either at the beginning of the passage or elsewhere. Sometimes the main idea may be found in the title of the passage. Oftentimes the main idea is not stated in the passage; the reader needs to determine it from the information or details in the passage. The main idea will become more and more obvious to a reader as detail after detail supports it. Some information in the passage may not be supporting, but most ideas and details will support the main idea. The main idea is filled out by the supporting details in a passage.

Denotative and connotative meaning of words

The *denotative meaning* of a word is the meaning that is found in a dictionary. It is the literal definition of a word. The connotative meaning is somewhat more subtle; it may also be listed in a dictionary, but after the literal meaning. The *connotative meaning* is what is suggested by or hinted at by a word, but not stated outright. The connotative meaning comes from the usage of the word. Its hidden meaning has come from personal experience. For instance, the words "lovely" and "exquisite" both mean "attractive," but "exquisite" suggests someone who is gorgeous or perfect-looking while "lovely" is less strong. When reading texts, you should always pay attention to words that have strong connotations because these words are a key to the author's opinion or point of view.

Connotative meaning of the word *animal* in the following sentence

"I can't believe what an animal you are; your room is a mess!"

The denotative meaning of the word *animal* is a living being that is not human. In this sentence, it is obvious that the author is not writing about nonhuman living beings. In this case, the connotative meaning of the word *animal* is being used: many animals allow themselves to be very dirty and eat messily. The feelings associated with the word *animal* (as used in this case) include: messy, dirty, wild, and improper. Using the connotative meaning, one could call a person an animal if he is acting in a messy, wild way. In this sentence, the person is called an animal because he keeps a messy room.

Analyzing a complex text

When you read a text, you need to pay attention. You need to watch for the introduction of ideas. You need to figure out how the ideas that are introduced are developed. When you read a complex text, it may be difficult to follow. Sometimes, it is hard to understand how one idea is linked to another idea. Sometimes, it helps to make an outline of a text. This will help you identify the main ideas. Then, you can figure out which ideas are supporting details. A complex text may also have vocabulary that you cannot understand. If you cannot figure out the meaning of certain words from the context, you can make a list of these words. Then, look them up in a dictionary. This will help you understand the meaning of the text.

Evaluate the following Supreme Court majority opinion in Dred Scott v. Sandford (1857)

"...We think they [people of African ancestry] are...not included, and were not intended to be included, under the word "citizens" in the Constitution, and can therefore claim none of the rights and privileges which that instrument provides for and secures to citizens of the United States. . ." Chief Justice Roger B. Taney.

Using the reasoning that the Founding Fathers believed that African Americans could not be viewed as citizens as defined in the US Constitution, and therefore had no rights before the Court, Chief Justice Taney's majority opinion ignited a firestorm of controversy in the already heated debate between pro- and anti-slavery advocates in the United States during the mid-19th century. Many opponents decried the chief justice's ruling as one that was motivated by politics. One result was that the US Congress could no longer regulate slavery anywhere. The Dred Scott Decision is viewed as one of a series of events that eventually pushed the country into the Civil War.

Analyze the Following Excerpt from Lincoln's Second Inaugural Address

"It may seem strange that any men should dare to ask a just God's assistance in wringing their bread from the sweat of other men's faces, but let us judge not, that we be not judged. The prayers of both could not be answered. That of neither has been answered fully..."

In this excerpt and in the address, Lincoln is talking about slavery. Like the majority of people of his time, Lincoln learned to read by studying the Bible. He makes frequent references to the Bible, and he often uses the rhetoric of the Bible to drive his point home. This is common in 19th century literary documents. When he says, "Wringing their bread from the sweat of other men's faces," he is paraphrasing from the Book of Genesis, which refers to physical work. Here, the word *bread* is used to refer to the wealth of the slave owners. Lincoln finds it strange that these slave owners should pray to the same God as those who do not own slaves for assistance in making money. He encourages his audience not to be hypocritical when he says, "let us judge not." This is a reference to the Book of Matthew of the Bible.

Evaluate the Purpose of the Following Excerpt from George Washington's Farewell Address

"The unity of government which constitutes you one people is also now dear to you. It is justly so, for it is a main pillar in the edifice of your real independence, the support of your tranquility at home, your peace abroad; of your safety; of your prosperity; of that very liberty which you so highly prize..."

This address given by the first president of the US when he announced that he did not want to run for re-election went over the groundwork that had established the new country. The passage stresses *the unity of government which constitutes you one people.* Washington truly believed that the US would be able to survive any attack, from without as well as from within, if it stayed with this principle. There is a hint that Washington foresaw the difficulties of holding together *the main pillar* (the different states) that were to come. His farewell address would go on to influence politicians and leaders for many years to come.

Index

A nonfiction book will typically have an index at the end so that the reader can easily find information about particular topics. An index lists the topics in alphabetical order. The names of people are listed with the last name first. For example, *Adams, John* would come before *Washington, George*. To the right of the entry, the relevant page numbers are listed. When a topic is mentioned over several pages, the index will often connect these pages with a dash. For instance, if the subject is mentioned from pages 35 to 42 and again on 53, then the index entry will be labeled as *35-42, 53*. Some entries will have subsets, which are listed below the main entry, indented slightly, and placed in alphabetical order. This is common for subjects that are discussed frequently in the book. For instance, in a book about Elizabethan drama, William Shakespeare will likely be an important topic. Beneath Shakespeare's name in the index, there might be listings for *death of, dramatic works of, life of*, etc. These more specific entries help the reader refine his search.

Dictionary

Dictionaries contain information about words. The words in a dictionary are listed in alphabetical order. A standard dictionary entry begins with a pronunciation guide for the word. The entry will also give the word's part of speech: that is, whether it is a noun, verb, adjective, etc. Some words can serve multiple functions in a sentence. For instance, the word *tough* is both an adjective meaning coarse or durable and a noun referring to a thug or a ruffian. The main component of a dictionary entry is the list of definitions. Some words have dozens of definitions. A good dictionary will also include the word's origins, including the language from which it is derived and its meaning in that language. This information is known as the word's etymology.

Headings and Subheadings

Many informative texts, especially textbooks, use headings and subheadings for organization. Headings and subheadings are typically printed in larger and bolder fonts, and are often in a different color than the main body of the text. Headings may be larger than subheadings. Also, headings and subheadings are not always complete sentences. A heading announces the topic that will be addressed in the text below. Headings are meant to alert the reader to what is about to come. Subheadings announce the topics of smaller sections within the entire section indicated by the heading. So, for instance, the heading of a section in a science textbook might be *AMPHIBIANS*, and within that section might be subheadings for *Frogs*, *Salamanders*, and *Newts*. Readers should always pay close attention to headings and subheadings, because they prime the brain for the information that is about to be delivered, and because they make it easy to go back and find particular details in a long text.

Line Graph

A line graph is typically used for measuring trends over time. It is set up along a vertical and a horizontal axis. The variables being measured are listed along the left side and the bottom side of the axes. Points are then plotted along the graph, such that they correspond with their values for each variable. For instance, imagine a line graph measuring a person's income for each month of the year. If the person earned $1500 in January, there would be a point directly above January, perpendicular to the horizontal axis, and directly to the right of $1500, perpendicular to the vertical axis. Once all of the lines are plotted, they are connected with a line from left to right. This line provides a nice visual illustration of the general trends. For instance, using the earlier example, if the line sloped up, it would be clear that the person's income had increased over the course of the year.

Identifying Specified Information from a Sample Listing of Items and Costs

Reading a table, for instance a menu or a set of movie listings is simple. In a typical menu format, the price is listed directly across from the item. However, in some cases all of the items in a category (desserts, for example) have the same price, and this price is given at the top of the section. Sometimes, the prices of additives (like 75 cents for cheese on a hamburger) are listed at the bottom of the section. In some restaurants, prices are listed without the dollar sign ($). Also, some restaurants automatically subtract a certain amount of money for the server's tip, and this information is usually listed at the bottom of the menu page. On a set of movie listings, it is typical for the times at which a picture is showing to be listed in chronological order, as in the following example: *Harold Goes to Mars – 1:15, 3:30, 5:45, 8, 10:30*. Note that times that are exactly on the hour do not include minutes. Also, in some places a period is used instead of a colon to separate hours and minutes.

Internet Sources

The Internet was once considered a poor place to find sources for an essay or article, but its credibility has improved greatly over the years. Still, students need to exercise caution when performing research online. The best sources are those affiliated with established institutions like universities, public libraries, and think tanks. Most newspapers are available online, and many of them allow the public to browse their archives. Magazines frequently offer similar services. When obtaining information from an unknown website, however, one must exercise considerably more caution. A website can be considered trustworthy if it is referenced by other sites that are known to be reputable. Also, credible sites tend to be properly maintained and frequently updated. A site is easier to trust when the author provides some information about him or herself, including some credentials that indicate expertise in the subject matter.

Topic and Summary Sentences

Topic and summary sentences are a convenient way to encapsulate the main idea of a text. In some textbooks and academic articles, the author will place a topic or summary sentence at the beginning of each section as a means of preparing the reader for what is to come. Research suggests that the brain is more receptive to new information when it has been prepared by the presentation of the main idea or some key words. The phenomenon is somewhat akin to the primer coat of paint that allows subsequent coats of paint to absorb more easily. A good topic sentence will be clear and not contain any jargon. When topic or summary sentences are not provided, many good readers may jot down their own so that they can find their place in a text and refresh their memory.

Fact and Opinion

Readers must always be conscious of the distinction between fact and opinion. A fact can be subjected to analysis and can be either proved or disproved. An opinion, on the other hand, is the author's personal feeling, which may not be alterable by research, evidence, or argument. If the author writes that the distance from New York to Boston is about two hundred miles, he is stating a fact. But if he writes that New York is too crowded, then he is giving an opinion because there is no objective standard for overpopulation. An opinion may be indicated by words like *believe*, *think*, or *feel*. Also, an opinion may be supported by facts: for instance, the author might give the population density of New York as a reason for why it is overcrowded. An opinion supported by fact tends to be more convincing. When authors support their opinions with other opinions, the reader is unlikely to be moved.

Biases and Stereotypes

Every author has a point of view, but when an author ignores reasonable counterarguments or distorts opposing viewpoints, he is demonstrating a bias. A bias is evident whenever the author is unfair or inaccurate in his presentation. Bias may be intentional or unintentional, but it should always alert the reader to be skeptical of the argument being made. It should be noted that a biased author may still be correct. However, the author will be correct in spite of her bias, not because of it. A stereotype is like a bias, except that it is specifically applied to a group or place. Stereotyping is considered to be particularly abhorrent because it promotes negative generalizations about people. Many people are familiar with some of the hateful stereotypes of certain ethnic, religious, and cultural groups. Readers should be very wary of authors who stereotype. These faulty assumptions typically reveal the author's ignorance and lack of curiosity.

False Analogy

A logical fallacy is a failure of reasoning. As a reader, it is important to recognize logical fallacies, because they diminish the value of the author's message. The four most common logical fallacies in writing are the false analogy, circular reasoning, false dichotomy, and overgeneralization. In a false analogy, the author suggests that two things are similar, when in fact they are different. This fallacy is often committed when the author is attempting to convince the reader that something unknown is like something relatively familiar. The author takes advantage of the reader's ignorance to make this false comparison. One example might be the following statement: *Failing to tip a waitress is like stealing money out of somebody's wallet*. Of course, failing to tip is very rude, especially when the service has been good, but people are not arrested for failing to tip as they would be for stealing money from a wallet. To compare stingy diners with thieves is a false analogy.

Circular Reasoning

Circular reasoning is one of the more difficult logical fallacies to identify because it is typically hidden behind dense language and complicated sentences. Reasoning is described as circular when it offers no support for assertions other than restating them in different words. Put another way, a circular argument refers to itself as evidence of truth. A simple example of circular argument is when a person uses a word to define itself, such as saying *Niceness is the state of being nice*. If the reader does not know what *nice* means, then this definition will not be very useful. In a text, circular reasoning is usually more complex. For instance, an author might say *Poverty is a problem for society because it creates trouble for people throughout the community*. It is redundant to say that poverty is a problem because it creates trouble. When an author engages in circular reasoning, it is often because he or she has not fully thought out the argument or cannot come up with any legitimate justifications.

False Dichotomy

One of the most common logical fallacies is the false dichotomy, in which the author creates an artificial sense that there are only two possible alternatives in a situation. This fallacy is common when the author has an agenda and wants to give the impression that his view is the only sensible one. A false dichotomy has the effect of limiting the reader's options and imagination. An example of a false dichotomy is the statement *You need to go to the party with me, otherwise you'll just be bored at home*. The speaker suggests that the only other possibility besides being at the party is being bored at home. This is not true, as it is perfectly possible to be entertained at home, or even to go somewhere other than the party. Readers should always be wary of the false dichotomy: when an author limits the alternatives, it is always wise to ask whether his argument valid.

Overgeneralization

Overgeneralization is a logical fallacy in which the author makes a claim that is so broad it cannot be proved or disproved. In most cases, overgeneralization occurs when the author wants to create an illusion of authority or when he is using sensational language to sway the opinion of the reader. For instance, in the sentence *Everybody knows that she is a terrible teacher*, the author makes an assumption that cannot really be believed. This kind of statement is made when the author wants to create the illusion of consensus when none actually exists. It may be that most people have a negative view of the teacher, but to say that *everybody* feels that way is an exaggeration. When a reader spots overgeneralization, she should become skeptical about the argument that is being made because an author will often try to hide a weak or unsupported assertion behind authoritative language.

Drawing Conclusions

Drawing conclusions from information implied within a passage requires confidence on the part of the reader. Implications are things the author does not state directly, but which can be assumed based on what the author does say. For instance, consider the following simple passage: "I stepped outside and opened my umbrella. By the time I got to work, the cuffs of my pants were soaked." The author never states that it is raining, but this fact is clearly implied. Conclusions based on implication must be well supported by the text. In order to draw a solid conclusion, a reader should have multiple pieces of evidence, or, if he only has one, must be assured that there is no other possible explanation than his conclusion. A good reader will be able to draw many conclusions from information implied by the text, which enriches the reading experience considerably.

A reader should always be drawing conclusions from the text, even if these conclusions are only provisional. It is always more comfortable to draw conclusions from information stated within a passage, rather than to draw them from mere implications. However, an author may provide some information and then describe a counterargument. The reader should be alert for direct statements that are subsequently rejected or weakened by the author. The reader should always read the entire passage before drawing conclusions. Many readers are trained to expect the author's conclusions at either the beginning or the end of the passage. However, many texts will not adhere to this format. The reader should be adept at outlining the information contained in the passage; an effective outline will reveal the structure of the passage, and will lead to solid conclusions.

Graphs, Tables, Charts, and Diagrams

In most cases, the work of interpreting information presented in graphs, tables, charts, and diagrams is done for the reader. The author will usually make explicit his or her reasons for presenting a certain set of data in such a way. However, an effective reader will avoid taking the author's claims for granted. Before considering the information presented in the graphic, the reader should consider whether the author has chosen the correct format for presentation, or whether the author has omitted variables or other information that might undermine his case. Interpreting the graphic itself is essentially an exercise in spotting trends. On a graph, for instance, the reader should be alert for how one variable responds to a change in the other. If education level increases, for example, does income increase as well? The same can be done for a table. Readers should be alert for values that break or exaggerate a trend; these may be meaningless outliers or indicators of a change in conditions.

Outline, Timeline, and Venn Diagram

Readers often use graphic organizers to recall information from a text. A graphic organizer may be an outline, timeline, mind-map, Venn diagram, or a multitude of other means of organizing information, all of which differ in format. For example, an outline uses Roman numerals, key points, and supporting points to organize information. A timeline is based on a series of dates or times that are an integral part of the story. A Venn diagram is used to compare ideas by placing them in separate circles; sometimes ideas overlap and are placed where the circles converge.

Any type of graphic organizer is a way to simplify information and take only the key points from the text. A graphic organizer such as a timeline may have an event listed for a corresponding date on the timeline, whereas an outline may have an event listed under a key point that occurs in the text. Each reader needs to create the type of graphic organizer that works the best for him or her in terms of being able to recall information from a story.

Effective Outline of Information Presented in a Paragraph or Message

To evaluate an outline, one must first assess the accuracy and relevance of the outline's title. The title must refer to the basic subject of the text, though it need not recapitulate the main idea. In most outlines, the main idea will be the first major section. An effective outline will have each major idea of the passage established as the head of a category. For instance, the most common outline format calls for the main ideas of the passage to be indicated with Roman numerals. In an effective outline of this kind, each of the main ideas will be represented by a Roman numeral and none of the Roman numerals will designate minor details or secondary ideas. Moreover, all supporting ideas and details should be placed in the appropriate place on the outline. An outline does not need to include every detail listed in the text, but it should feature all of those that are central to the argument or message. Each of these details should be listed under the appropriate main idea.

Review Video: Outlining as an Aid to Drawing Conclusions
Visit mometrix.com/academy and enter code: 584445

Pie Chart

A pie chart is effective at showing how a single entity is divided into parts. For instance, a pie chart would be appropriate for demonstrating how the federal budget is spent. A large wedge of the pie would be devoted to military spending, a smaller wedge to foreign aid, and so on. Pie charts indicate how the parts of a whole relate to one another, as well as to the whole itself. They are not effective at demonstrating the relationships between parts of different wholes. For example, it would not be as helpful to use a pie chart to compare the respective amounts of state and federal spending devoted to infrastructure, since these values are only meaningful in the context of the entire budget.

Types of Logical Organization that are Frequently Used in Research

There are six major types of logical organization that are frequently used:

1. Illustrations may be used to support the thesis. Examples are the most common form of this organization.
2. A series of definitions identifying what something is or is not is another way of organization. What are the characteristics of the topic?
3. Dividing or classifying information into separate items according to their similarities is a common and effective organizing method.
4. Comparing, focusing on the similarities of things, and contrasting, highlighting the differences between things, together form an excellent tool to use with certain kinds of information.
5. Cause and effect is a simple tool to logically understand relationships between things. A phenomenon may be traced to its causes for organizing a subject logically.
6. Problem and solution is a simple and effective manner of logically organizing material. It is very commonly used and lucidly presents information.

Adding Visual Elements to a Document

Visual elements—such as charts, graphs, tables, photographs, maps, and diagrams—are useful in conveying information vividly and in a summary form.

Flow charts and pie charts are useful in helping readers follow a process or showing numerical information in graphic style. Tables are less stimulating but offer devices for summarizing information.

Diagrams are useful and sometimes necessary in scientific writing, to explain chemical formulas, for example.

Visual elements may be placed in a document close to the textual discussion or put in an appendix, labeled, and referred to in a text. Sometimes page layout makes it difficult to position visuals in optimum proximity to the corresponding text. In these cases, visuals may be placed later in the text, and readers told where they can find them. Software may be used to help the text flow around the visual for maximum impact.

Post hoc fallacy

Tracing cause and effect can be a complicated matter. Because of the complexity involved, writers often oversimplify it. A common error is to assume that because one event follows another, the first is the cause of the second. This common fallacy is known as post hoc, from the Latin meaning "after this, therefore because of this."

A post hoc fallacy could run like this: "Since Abner Jones returned to the Giants lineup, the team has much better morale." The fact that Jones returned to the lineup may or may not have had an effect on team morale. The writer must show there is a cause and effect relationship between Jones's return and team morale. It is not enough to note that one event followed another. It must be proved beyond a reasonable doubt that morale was improved by the return of Jones to the lineup. The two may be true but do not necessarily follow a cause-and-effect pattern.

Vocabulary Development

Language Usage

Latin is an ancient language. It does not change. But English, like any modern language, may change over time. New words are always being introduced into the English language. Words are adapted from other languages. Examples of adapted words are taco, pizza, and karaoke. Usage, which is a matter of convention, can also change and evolve over time. It is not always clear what the correct form is, since there are sometimes two possibilities. For instance, the use of the subjunctive is much less prevalent today than it was in the past. The answer to the question of whether it is acceptable to begin a question with the word "and" or "but" has also changed. Years ago, this was strictly against usage rules, but it is now common practice in less formal texts.

Affixes and Roots

A root word is the original word, before it is added onto. An affix is a prefix, infix, or suffix that is added onto a root word. Often, the affixes in the English language come from Latin or Greek origins. A prefix is added before a root word, an infix is added to the middle of a root word, and a suffix is added to the end of a root word. When you look at the meaning of a root word and the meaning of any affixes added to the root word, you can figure out the approximate meaning of the word. For example, the root word "like" means to enjoy. The prefix "dis-"means not. The reader can therefore see that "dislike" means to not enjoy.

Etymology

Etymology is the study of words. It specifically focuses on the origins of words: how they have developed over time and between languages. Language is made up of words from different cultures and areas of the world. Some words we use today mean something completely different from what they meant hundreds of years ago. Words are constantly being redefined, changed, and created. New words appear as technology increases. Some words are formed by combining root words with prefixes and suffixes. Students who must improve verbal ability for standardized testing can do so by studying common prefixes and suffixes. By understanding the prefix *pre*, a student increases their chances of understanding words like *predate*. The prefix *pre* means "before", so it can be reasoned that *predate* means to date something in advance, such as predating a check.

Prefixes

Prefixes are a group of letters that are placed in front of a root word. When combined with a root word, a prefix alters the meaning of the original word. For example, consider the prefix *sub-*. *Sub-* means under, below, or less than. Knowing this, one can combine the prefix *sub-* with a variety of root words and understand what each means. The word *terrain* refers to a piece of land or ground. By adding the word *sub-* to *terrain* one creates the word *sub terrain*. Based on the definition of each part of this word, one can assume that *sub terrain* refers to something that is below or underground.

EXAMPLES OF SOME PREFIXES

Prefix	Meaning	Sample words
a-	not or without	amoral, atypical, and atheist
ab-	away from	abstain, abnormal, and absent
acro-	high, top, or tip	acrophobia, acronym, and acrobat
ad-	toward or to	addition, adhesive, and admonish
alt-	high	altitude, altar, and altimeter
ante-	before	antemortem, antecedent, and antebellum
anti-	against	antidote, antibody, and antifreeze
audi-	to hear	audible, audience, and audition
auto-	self	autobiography, autoimmune, and automotive
be-	by or near	beside, begrudge, and belie
bene-	good or well	benefit, benevolent, and benediction
bi-	two	bilateral, bilingual, and bipartisan
chron-	time	chronology, chronic, and chronicle
circum-	around or about	circumnavigate, circumstantial, and circumference
co-	with or together	cosign, cooperate, and coworker
com-	together	combine, component, and compatible
contra-	against	contraband, contradict, and contrary
counter-	opposite	counterintelligence, counterintuitive, and counterproductive
de-	from, down, or away	degrade, despite, and detach
demo-	people	demographic, demonstrate, and democracy
dia-	through, across, or between	diameter, diagonal, and diaphragm
dis-	away, not, or negative	dissuade, disengage, and disdain
dyn-	power	dynamic, dynasty, and dynamite
ecto-	outside or external	ectoplasm, ectosphere, and ectopic
endo-	inside	endoscopic, endothermal, and endogenous
equi-	equal	equidistant, equivalent, and equinox
ex-	out of or former	exponent, extent, and examine
extra-	beyond	extraterrestrial, extraordinary, and extrasensory
hetero-	other	heterosexual, heterogony, and heterochromatic
homo-	same	homogenous, homosexual, and homonym
hyper-	over or above	hypersensitive, hyperbole, and hypertext
hypo-	below or less than	hypoglycemia, hypothermia, and hypodermic
in-	not	insane, innate, and inorganic
infra-	below or beneath	infrastructure, infrared, and infrasonic
inter-	between	intercept, interoffice, and intercede
intra-	within	intravenous, intracranial, and intraorbital
macro-	large	macrobiotic, macrophage, and macroscopic
mal-	bad	malady, maladjusted, and malfunction
mega-	large	megaphone, megabyte, and megalopolis
meso-	middle	Mesolithic, mesosphere, and mesoderm
micro-	small	microscope, micrometer, and microprocessor
mid-	middle	midday, midline, and midsummer
mini-	small	minivan, miniscule, and minimum
mis-	wrong	misfit, mismatch, and mistake
multi-	many	multicolor, multiply, and multinational

neo-	new	neoclassic, Neolithic, and neoplasm
non-	not	nondescript, nonchalant, and nonfiction
ob-	against	object, obscure and obstinate
omni-	all	omnipotent, omniscient, and omnivorous
over-	excessive	overindulgent, overage, and oversensitive
para-	beside	paranormal, parametric, and paraprofessional
peri-	around	perinatal, perimeter, and periscope
phot-	light	photograph, photosynthesize, and photon
poly-	many	polynomial, polydactyl, and polygamy
post-	after or later	postmortem, posterior, and postlude
pre-	before	premonition, predecessor, and preeminent
pro-	supporting	probiotic, proliferate, and procreate
pseudo-	false	pseudonym, pseudonarcotic, and pseudomorph
re-	again	repeat, reverberate, and redirect
retro-	backward	retrofit, retrospect, and retroactive
sanct-	holy	sanction, sanctuary, and sanctimonious
semi-	half	semifinal, semiannual, and semicircle
socio-	social or society	sociopath, socioeconomic, and sociocultural
sub-	under	subject, subside, and submarine
super-	above	supernatural, supersede, and superficial
supra-	above	supraorbital, suprarenal, and supraliminal
syn-	together	synergy, synthesis, and synchronize
tele-	from a distance or from afar	telephone, telepathy, and teleport
therm-	heat	thermal, thermodynamic, and thermometer
trans-	across	transcontinental, transaction, and transfer
ultra-	beyond	ultraviolet, ultrarapid, and ultrasafe
un-	not	undecided, unjust, and unforgettable
under-	beneath	underused, underage, and underlie
vita-	life	vitamins, vital, and vitalism
with-	against or back	withhold, withstand, and withdraw

SUFFIXES

A suffix is a group of letters placed at the end of a root word. Suffixes can perform one of two possible functions: they can be used to create a new word or they can shift the tense of a word without changing its original meaning. For example, the suffix *-ability* can be added to the end of the word *account* to form the new word *accountability. Account* means a written narrative or description of events, while *accountability* means the state of being liable. The suffix *-ed* can be added to *account* to form the word *accounted*, which simply shifts the word from present tense to past tense.

The suffix of a word can be extremely important in telling a reader what function the word has in a sentence. Certain endings are used to make a stem an adjective; others are used to make a stem a noun. For instance, the root *consider* has many forms. It becomes a noun—*consideration*—with the addition of *–ation*. It becomes an adjective—*considerate*—with the addition of the suffix *-ate.* The adverb *considerately* can be made from the adjective *considerate* by adding *–ly*. This is a simple yet sophisticated method of figuring out what part of speech a word is.

The root word for *absolution* is *absolute*. The suffix *-tion* indicates that the word is a noun. The root could be combined with other suffixes to make other parts of speech as well. Add an *–ly* and you have the adverb *absolutely*. This word is a noun in its root form (*absolute*), so no change is needed to it. To make the verb *absolve*, the suffix *–ve* is added. This word is irregular, since most roots tend to be in verb form. It is important to be able to analyze a word, not just for its etymology, but also to determine what part of speech the word might be.

Certain suffixes require that the root word be modified. If the suffix begins with a vowel, such as -*ing*, and the root word ends in the letter *e*, the letter *e* must be dropped before adding the suffix. For example, the word *write* will become *writing*. If the suffix begins with a consonant instead of a vowel, the letter *e* at the end of the root word does not need to be dropped. For example, *hope* would become *hopeless*. The only exceptions to this specific rule are the words *judgment*, *acknowledgment*, and *argument*. If a root word ends in the letter *y* and is preceded by a consonant, change the *y* to an *i* before adding the suffix. This is the case for all suffixes, except those that begin with the letter *i*. For example, *plenty* becomes *plentiful*.

Sometimes adding a suffix can change the spelling of a word. If the suffix begins with a vowel, the final consonant of the root word must be doubled. This rule applies only if the root word has one syllable or if the accent is on the last syllable. For example, when adding the suffix *-ery* to the root word *rob*, the final word becomes *robbery*. The letter *b* is doubled because *rob* is only one syllable. However, when adding the suffix *-able* to the root word *profit*, the final word becomes *profitable*. The letter *t* is not doubled because the root word *profit* has two syllables. Spelling is not changed when the suffixes *-less*, *-ness*, *-ly*, or *-en* are used. The only exception to this rule is when the root word ends in *y* and the suffix *-ness* or *-ly* will be added. In this case, the *y* changes to an *i*. For example, *happy* becomes *happily*.

EXAMPLES OF SOME SUFFIXES

Suffix	Meaning	Sample words
-al	related to or process of	congenital, spatial, subliminal
-ance	the condition of	continuance, dominance, compliance
-ate	having	satiate, radiate, alienate
-ation	the process of or action	duplication, contamination, starvation
-cy	the condition or state of	pregnancy, bankruptcy, supremacy
-ability	having an inclination for	predictability, culpability, deniability
-able	worthy of an act	conceivable, valuable, laughable
-ac	pertaining to	cardiac, insomniac, maniac
-acy	having the quality of	efficacy, accuracy, democracy
-age	a collection or condition	bondage, footage, percentage
-ese	relating to or having the characteristics of	legalese, Japanese, Balinese
-ial	pertaining to	colonial, tutorial, spatial
-ian	relating or belonging to	median, physician, statistician
-ing	conveys an action	calling, telling, shopping
-ist	one who performs an action	pianist, typist, sadist
-ed	the past tense of a verb	walked, cried, dated
-en	to cause to be	blacken, weaken, tighten
-ence	the state or condition of	independence, emergence, existence
-er	one who performs	dancer, entertainer, server
-ery	the state or place of	surgery, nunnery, bribery
-ize	to cause to be	immobilize, standardize, prioritize
-less	without	powerless, joyless, fearless

-logy	study of	theology, psychology, archaeology
-ment	action or process of	merriment, banishment, replacement
-meter	measurement of	thermometer, perimeter, centimeter
-ious	full of or having	precocious, noxious, vicious
-ish	characteristic of	prudish, Amish, foolish
-ism	action or practice of	alcoholism, fascism, terrorism
-ity	the action or process of	abnormality, partiality, oddity
-ive	performing an action	impassive, decisive, demonstrative
-osis	conveys a condition	mitosis, osmosis, neurosis
-s/-es	indicates that a word is plural	tomatoes, wagons, boys
-ship	the state or quality of	hardship, ownership, apprenticeship
-some	full of	lonesome, worrisome, tiresome
-tion	an action or condition	contrition, abolition, superstition
-ty	quality or condition of	vanity, sanctity, loyalty
-ness	quality or condition	fullness, happiness, sadness
-oid	resembling	humanoid, asteroid, spheroid
-or	state of	behavior, demeanor, fervor
-ory	characterized by	auditory, statutory, mandatory
-ose	full of or possessing	varicose, comatose, sucrose
-cide	to kill	infanticide, fratricide, genocide
-ectomy	to cut away	mastectomy, vasectomy, appendectomy
-ite	one connected with	graphite, trilobite, hematite
-ia	an act or state	insomnia, mania, hypoglycemia
-phobia	illogical fear of	aquaphobia, arachnophobia, claustrophobia

EXAMPLES OF SOME ROOT WORDS

Root	Meaning	Sample words
ac	to do	action, active, activity
ag	to do	agenda, agree, agitate
agri	farm	agriculture, agribusiness
anthropo	man	anthropology, anthropomorphic
aqua	water	aquatic, aquaphilia
aud	hearing	audio, auditory
auto	self	autopilot, autopsy
biblio	book	bibliography, biblioclast
bio	life	biology, biometrics
capit	head	capital, capitulate
fer	carry	ferry, transfer
fract	break	fracture, fraction
frater	brother	fraternity, fraternal
gen	produce	generate, antigen
geo	earth	geography, geology
graph	picture or writing	epigraph, pictograph
hemo	blood	hemoglobin, hemophilia
homo	man	homogenous, homicide
hydr	water	hydraulic, hydration
ject	throw	trajectory, inject

cede	go	recede, intercede
celer	speed	accelerate, decelerate
chron	time	chronology, chronic
cide	kill	infanticide, pesticide
clued	close	include, preclude, conclude
cog	knowledge	cognizant, precognition
ded	give	dedicate
dent	tooth	dental, dentist
duc	lead	induct, induce
fac	make or do	manufacture, facilitate
mort	death	mortuary, mortician
mute	change	mutation, commute
naut	sailor or ship	nautical, astronaut
nounce	declare	announce, pronounce
ped	foot	pedicure, pedal
philo	love	philosophy, hydrophilia
port	carry	portal, porter
psych	mind	psychology, psychic
reg	rule	regulate, regal
rupt	break	interrupt, rupture
jud	right	judge, judicial
junct	join	junction, conjunctivitis
juris	justice or law	jurisdiction
lect	read	lecture, elect
logue	speech	dialogue, monologue
loq	speak	soliloquy
lude	play	interlude, delude
manu	hand	manuscript, manual

Writing and Language

Writing Conventions

Composition Planning

Before you begin writing, you must spend some time planning what you are going to say. However, you should never assume that you can create a comprehensive outline in advance of a composition, because you will inevitably revise and expand your message during the writing process.

To begin with, consider the basic characteristics of your writing assignment: that is, the topic, length, format, intent, resources, and audience. Some of these characteristics may be undetermined in the beginning. It is important to consider whether your chosen topic can be covered effectively in the required space. A topic may need to be expanded or narrowed in order to fit the assigned length. Also, you should consider whether your topic is appropriate to the writing task and audience. If you are being asked to incorporate external references (i.e., if you are being asked to write a research paper), you should determine whether there will be enough (or too many) references for you to complete your task.

Listing and Freewriting

Often, writers find that the hardest thing about writing is getting started. There are a number of exercises that can help you get "into" your topic during the planning stage. Many writers begin by creating a list of ideas related to the subject. These ideas can be facts, opinions, or even questions. The important thing is to get them down on paper so that they can be examined critically. The mechanical act of composing such a list helps the brain organize itself and chart a path for writing. Some writers make a list on the computer and then rearrange the items until a vague structure emerges. Then, they set to work on a more detailed outline.

Freewriting is another useful planning exercise in which you simply write as fast as you can about your subject until you run out of things to say. A free-write is not expected to be organized or even grammatical. It is just a way to get things down on the page so that they can be evaluated and ordered.

Notes and Concept Maps

If you are planning a research paper or a response to a piece of writing, you will probably need to take some notes during the planning process. As you read the relevant texts, jot down any crucial ideas or questions that emerge. After you have completed your reading, these notes will be used to form your outline. Your notes tell you what was most interesting, essential, or problematic about the text. You can even make your notes into a list, and then rearrange them into the structure of a response or research paper.

Some writers, especially those with a visual bent, write down the main ideas and terms from the text and arrange them according to their relationships. This diagram is called a concept map. It depicts the general structure of the topic being addressed. Oftentimes, the creation of a concept map helps a writer discover surprising connections.

Outlines

Toward the end of the planning stage, you should construct an outline. The degree of structure and detail in your outline will depend on the nature of the assignment and your work to this point. An outline should mimic the organization of the composition. Its purpose is to order and prioritize the main elements of the piece. The outline should begin with the thesis statement, which is a short summation of the main idea. Underneath the main idea, the most important supporting ideas should be listed. Under each of these, and slightly indented, should be a list of supporting details. These details may also be supported by further information. The various elements of the structure (supporting ideas details, etc.) should be organized with Roman numerals, numbers, and letters. In the most common outline structure, the most general ideas are assigned Roman numerals (I, II, III, etc.), supporting ideas are assigned capital letters (A, B, C, etc.), and even more specific points are identified with numbers. An extremely detailed and complex outline may also need to use lower-case numerals and letters.

Drafting a Thesis Statement

The thesis statement expresses the main idea of the composition. Every idea, argument, and detail in the composition should relate in some way to the thesis. When drafting the thesis statement, you must take care that you are general enough to include everything that is to follow, but specific enough that you are making a clear point. As much as possible, the thesis statement should be a short, declarative statement that can be evaluated by the reader. A thesis statement should not be a vague, subjective claim ("The Principal is basically a nice guy"); it should be more precise and testable ("The Principal's policies demonstrate his care for students"). The thesis statement should suggest the content of the rest of the piece, so that your audience will know what to expect.

Final Proofreading

After your paper has been fully revised and edited, you should perform a final proofreading. This is a slow, careful check for typographical and grammatical errors. By this point in the writing process, you should be finished evaluating and revising the content and structure of the paper. The final proofread is more targeted at small errors that will distract the reader. At present, the greatest enemy of effective proofreading is the spell-check feature in word-processing programs. Too many students believe that this function saves them the trouble of performing a final proofread. However, spell-checkers are terrible at spotting errors of grammar and diction. If you use the wrong word by accident, your spell-check will never know (unless of course you misspell the incorrect word). Many writers find proofreading to be very dull, but it is vastly preferable to the embarrassment of turning in an essay with obvious mistakes.

Literary Tropes

To engage and entertain the reader, many writers will use literary tropes, or figurative language. Some common examples of tropes are metaphors, similes, understatement, and irony. All of these tropes can be employed to good effect, but they must be appropriate to the subject. For instance, a metaphor (a statement in which one thing is described in terms of another – *The moon was a jagged knife*) can be a great way of relating an unfamiliar subject to something with which the reader is more familiar. However, metaphors have a tendency to become excessively florid and complex, which can distract from the discussion at hand. When dealing with a dry subject, figurative language should be used sparingly. In persuasive and interpretive writing, on the other hand, figurative language can be a great way to establish a tone and engage the imagination of the reader.

Validity, Reliability, and Relevance of Primary and Secondary Sources

Research papers depend on information taken from primary and secondary sources. A primary source derives directly from the topic, with no intermediation. Examples of primary sources include diaries, eyewitness accounts, videos, letters, legislative documents, and experimental data. Secondary sources, on the other hand, are commentaries or interpretations of primary sources. Some familiar secondary sources include books and articles of history and literary criticism. When incorporating these sources into your writing, be sure that you only use those that are valid, reliable, and relevant. The validity of a source is indicated by the extent to which it is confirmed and echoed in other works. When a source is considered valid, it will be cited in other texts on the same subject. The reliability of a source is the extent to which it consistently supports the point you are using it to make. A work would be unreliable, for instance, if it consistently makes statements only to undermine them later. The relevance of a source is the extent to which it applies to the subject of your essay.

Interpretation of an Expository or Literary Text

To write an effective interpretation of an expository or literary text, it is usually necessary to limit your interest to a particular aspect of the text. In general, an interpretation may focus on the topic (story); major characters or events; setting; structure; point of view; and use of language. This last item includes the author's rhetorical style, use of figurative language, and tone. An interpretation should both describe the text and elaborate upon it. For instance, in an interpretation of a short story's characters, you should introduce the important figures, explain how they are portrayed throughout the story, and then discuss what the author might be trying to demonstrate through his or her handling of the characters. An interpretation of an expository text's structure should outline the basic elements of the presentation, and then evaluate their effectiveness.

Addressing Literary Style and Rhetorical Effects

Many literary interpretations fail because they merely identify the author's literary methods, and do not analyze and evaluate them. An interpretation should always move beyond identification to evaluation and, in some cases, judgment. Of course, literary works are often ambiguous and complex, so it may not be appropriate to render a final verdict. An interpretation is successful when it takes a provisional position while maintaining respect for the ambiguities of the work. Ambiguity is the presence of multiple, somewhat inconsistent truths in a literary work. It should not be confused with vagueness. Great literary works are not equivalent to treatises; that is, they do not make declarations or arguments. Instead, they attempt to show life in all of its contradictory and messy reality. A literary interpretation ought to make claims, but it should also recognize that literary works often provide more questions than answers.

Essential Characteristics of a Persuasive Essay

A persuasive essay tries to convince the reader to adopt the viewpoint of the writer on a particular issue. In order for this to work, the essay needs to be on a topic that is susceptible to reason. An essay like "Chocolate ice cream is the best" will never work, because it depends on taste rather than logic. Some people will always prefer vanilla. A better topic for a persuasive essay would be, "Ice cream parlors should come up with more varieties of chocolate ice cream," because this assertion could be supported by market research and cost information. A persuasive essay should always demonstrate a keen understanding of its audience. The writer should consider the interests, prior knowledge, and learning style of the audience when constructing his or her argument.

Expert Opinions

A persuasive essay will often use examples to illustrate the main points of its argument, but these examples can as easily undermine the argument if they are chosen and presented improperly. Indeed, examples are most effective when they complement facts. When they are used, examples should be obviously appropriate to the argument. They are a good way to make dry facts and statistics more interesting or comprehensible for the reader.

Expert opinions can also be useful for this purpose, though they must be included with care. The expert should have a title or credential that clearly indicates his or her knowledge and experience in the topic. Also, the quote or reference from the expert should clearly be appropriate to the argument. If the expert quote does not actually support the argument, but is merely recorded to lend an air of sophistication, it should not be included. Also, the source material should always be provided to the reader.

Repetition

Authors use rhetorical schemes to emphasize, to draw analogies, and to engage the reader. A common technique is repetition, in which the author uses the same word several times quickly, either to call its meaning into question or to draw emphasis. Consider the sentence "They called him a slave, he thought of himself as a slave, and his prospects were no better than those of a slave." The repetition of the word *slave* mimics the plodding, hopeless nature of slavery, but also causes the reader to focus on the word and consider whether it is really appropriate here.

Proofreading One's Writing

When proofreading one's writing, it is important to look for a number of things. One should proofread their text at least twice, each time with a different focus: editing and revision. The first time the paper is proofread, it should be revised, looking for ways to improve the organization, clarity of ideas, word choice, and sentence structure and variety. Once finished with the revisions, the paper will need to be proofread again, making sure it is mechanically correct, keeping an eye out for misspelled words, errors in verb usage or tense, mistakes in comma use, and incorrect capitalization and punctuation.

Revise the Follow Sentence to Make It Correct

The members of the committee votes on important budget issues.

This sentence has an error in subject-verb agreement. In a correct sentence, the subject and verb need to agree in number. This sentence has a plural subject (members of the committee) and a singular verb (votes). There are two ways to revise the sentence, depending on what the author really means. If it is correct as a plural subject, it would change to:

> The members of the committee <u>vote</u> on important budget issues.

If it is instead correct to have a singular subject, it would change to:

> <u>Each member</u> of the committee votes on important budget issues.

Revise the Follow Sentence to Make It Correct

Did anyone leave their jacket at the park when we were there this afternoon?

This sentence has an error in pronoun-antecedent agreement. This means that the pronoun and its antecedent do not match in either number or gender. In this case, *anyone* is the pronoun. It is singular, but the antecedent *their* is plural. This is incorrect because there is no number match. To correct the error, the antecedent must be made singular. Here is the correct version of the sentence:

> Did anyone leave <u>his</u> jacket at the park when we were there this afternoon?

Revise the Follow Sentence to Make It Correct

The *author* of the book, Twilight on the Mississippi, Ronald Davies, loves doing book readings on college campuses.

This sentence needs to be revised to use italics correctly. In this case, the word "author" is italicized but does not need to be set off in any way. Italics are used to distinguish a word or phrase from the rest of the sentence. They are used in the following situations: titles of books, foreign words, words of words, names of vehicles, or for emphasis. The word "author" does not need to be emphasized, but the title of the book should be italicized. Here is the corrected version of the sentence:

> The author of the book, *Twilight on the Mississippi*, Ronald Davies, loves doing book readings on college campuses.

Revise the Follow Sentence to Make it Correct

When we went to the beach, we spent the whole day swimming in the water, building sand castles, and we took walks along the beach.

This sentence does not have parallel structure with the items in comma series. The phrases *swimming in the water*, *building sand castles*, and *we took walks* should all be parallel in verb structure. In order to revise the sentence, the phrases in the comma series need to be made parallel.

One way to correctly revise the sentence is:

> When we went to the beach, we spent the whole day swimming in the water, building sand castles, and taking walks along the beach.

Here is another correct revision:

> When we spent the day at the beach, we swam in the water, built sand castles, and took walks along the beach.

Parallelism

Parallelism means writing with a parallel structure, meaning all nouns, verbs, and phrases should have the same structure. For example, in the following sentence, the verbs are parallel:

> John runs fast and plays hard.

Both *runs* and *plays* are simple third person present tense verbs. Parallelism also applies to phrases. An example of this is:

> My hobbies are *playing* the piano, *running* marathons, and *reading* books.

If the sentence was written without parallel structure for the verb phrases, the sentence would seem awkward and disjointed (i.e., My hobbies are *playing* the piano, *running* marathons and *to read* books).

Fragment

A *fragment* is an incomplete sentence or thought that cannot stand on its own. Fragments are missing either nouns or verbs and are very confusing to the reader because the thought is not complete. When revising one's writing, the document needs to be read carefully to ensure any fragments are caught and revised. One needs to identify whether the fragment is missing a noun or verb and replace it. Sometimes, a fragment is the beginning part of the next sentence. In this case, the two can be combined in order to make one complete thought.

Clarifying a Thought or Creating an Interpretation

When discussing a text, it is important to use elements of the text to strengthen one's position. If one needs to clarify something they read, they should go back to the text, reread it, and use the text to make sure they have a firm understanding of the point the author is trying to make. Similarly, when one is interpreting a piece of text, you're the interpretation needs to be based upon the text itself. Using supporting evidence from the text strengthens the interpretation because it is made clear that the original text was thoroughly read and that the interpretation was based on the details and facts within it. Elements of text that can be used in a response include: facts, details, statistics, and direct quotations from the text.

Sentences Using the Gerund, Infinitive, and Present Participle Forms of the Verb "To Read"

A gerund ends in -ing and is used as a noun in the sentence. An infinitive is a singular verb preceded by the word "to." A participle ends in -ing and forms the progressive tense of the verb.

Gerund – All of the children listened carefully to the librarian's <u>reading</u> of the story.

Infinitive – I never knew that she liked <u>to read</u> mystery novels.

Participle –He is <u>reading</u> while he waits for the doctor to see him.

Integrating Various Sources of Information That Are Presented in Diverse Formats and Media in Order to Make Informed Decisions and Solve Problems

There are many different sources of information. On the Internet, there are multiple sites (some more reliable than others) where print information as well as charts and other graphic organizers are available to all. In addition, there are hard copy and online journals, textbooks, magazines, and newspapers; researchers are often overwhelmed with information. It is best to choose only the sources that can be verified or are from a credible author or organization. This information must then be analyzed to see how consistent it is and whether valid discrepancies exist, and why. After, it can be used in a presentation or a discussion.

Formal Style

A formal style is used when writing essays, both persuasive and informative. This style helps the writer achieve objectivity and keep the language precise. Formal writing consists of complex words and sentences; sentence fragments should be avoided unless they are being used for a specific reason. The tone of the writing is serious. The third person is always used, not the first or second person. An active voice is preferred because it projects more energy than a passive voice. Contractions are not used in formal writing. Sentences should be grammatically correct, as should the spelling and punctuation. When writing, reread and edit your passage several times to improve it. Vary the kinds of sentences and make sure that your ideas follow a logical order as well.

Appropriate Transitions

The use of appropriate transition words helps to clarify the relationships between ideas and concepts and creates a more cohesive passage. A good writer knows that such words and phrases serve to indicate the relationship between ideas and concepts. Words or phrases that show causality between ideas include "as a result," "consequently" and "therefore." Words that show a compare-and-contrast relationship include "however," "on the other hand," "in contrast" and "but." When introducing examples of different concepts, words such as "namely," "for example" and "for instance" act as transition words. Transition words such as "foremost," "primarily," "secondly," "former" and "latter" can be used when showing the order of importance of ideas or concepts.

Precise Language

An author's precise language can help a reader gain insight into a story that an author has written. Precise language, including phrases and sensory language, helps the reader imagine a place, situation, or person in the way that the writer wishes. The details that an author uses to describe a setting or character will help bring a story to life and convey exactly what the author envisions. Details of what characters do, the setting, and the events in a narrative help create a lively and thought-provoking story. Sensory language helps convey the mood and feeling of the setting and characters and will bring insight into the theme of a narrative. When reading, take special care to understand the range of language that an author employs in order to better comprehend the meaning.

Conclusion to a Narrative

The conclusion of a narrative is extremely important because it shapes the entire story and creates the theme that the author was attempting to convey. The conclusion of a narrative is the resolution of the problem that is faced by the characters. Some conclusions may be tragic, such as those in the many classic tragedies; other endings may be lighthearted, much in the style of classic comedies. Modern stories tend to have endings that are more complex than the clear-cut endings of classic literature. They often leave the reader without a clear sense of how a character fares at the end. Nonetheless, this element tells the reader that life is not always clear in its conclusions, which is a lesson that many writers strive to teach.

Gathering Relevant Information from Multiple Print and Digital Sources

When conducting research, your primary job is to list the kind of information you are looking for and then create a list of keywords to use for a search in multiple print and digital sources. Take extensive notes, noting the source that each bit of information comes from. Be sure to check on the reliability and credibility of each source. Journals, textbooks, magazines, and newspapers are all useful sources. Also, always verify how timely, accurate and credible your sources and information are. Dismiss any sources that seem questionable. When writing your report, you may paraphrase, but do not copy information down directly because that constitutes plagiarism. Use fresh language and attempt to rewrite the details and other information in your own language. Use the Modern Language Association (MLA) guidelines for all citations.

Topic Introduction

An informational or explanatory text should introduce the topic featured in the text. You can accomplish this by using a topic sentence followed by details supporting your thesis. Another tactic involves referring to a current event, even if your topic refers to something in history. Ideas should be organized in a logical manner, with supporting details coming right after a main concept. Connections can be made between concepts by using connecting words such as *however, since,* and *as a result.* Distinctions between ideas also should be made clear and can be signaled by words and phrases such as *but* or *on the other hand.* Furthermore, you can choose whether to include a specific relationship such as cause and effect, question and answer, or problem and solution.

Concluding Statement

While a good beginning is essential, equally important to an essay, lecture, or other presentation is an effective conclusion. A good concluding statement should sum up the overall intention of the text and serve to "wrap up" the presentation so the reader is aware that you have made a logical ending to your thesis and has closure. Ideally the conclusion would review the most important points made in the presentation, the reasoning employed, and the supporting arguments for this reasoning. The conclusion builds a bridge between the presentation and the audience that helps to reassert the importance of the effort and impact the viewer's memory favorably. A good conclusion allows the reader to sit back and weigh the overall impact of the presentation.

Dialogue, Pacing, Plot Lines, and Descriptions

Authors use a variety of techniques to bring to life their narratives. Authors employ dialogue to help develop characters. The words characters speak give endless clues into their personalities as well as their conflicts and needs. Dialogue also gives the reader a sense of what is happening. Pacing is another valuable technique. Rather than have the action move along at the same pace, writers change pace according to the effect they want to achieve. To build mystery or drama, a fast pace works well; a slow pace often sets the stage before something eventful occurs. Pace is the rhythm of a narrative. Plot lines are equally important, because they provide structure in the narrative. Description can create a setting or give insight into characters. They help the reader visualize what is happening.

Coherent Sequence of Events

A narrative's sequence of events usually emerges in order, because this is the most straightforward way to create a coherent sequence, which will not leave the reader confused. Such a structure provides a natural flow in the narrative, revealed through the dialogue and plot. A coherent sequence enhances a story, and it should never seem forced or unnatural. On the other hand, some writers change the natural order with a literary device called flashback. A flashback occurs when the writer chooses to go forward in time and then follow the natural sequence. Properly done, the flashback makes sense in the context of the story. Flashbacks can add a sense of mystery or suspense to a narrative as well as provide the reader with another literary device, foreshadowing. Nonetheless, chronological narration is used more frequently.

Planning, Revising, Editing, and Reviewing a Text to Make It Reach a Specific Audience

When beginning to write, you should develop a plan about what you want to discuss and the points you want to make. An outline can prove helpful if you are writing a nonfiction piece. If you are writing a narrative, you might want to make a story map. Next, you should write a first draft. Once you have finished the writing, you should put it aside for a time. When you come back to it, you will see it with fresh eyes and will see more easily what needs to be changed or revised. After you make the revisions and put the writing aside again, then reread the writing and begin to edit it for any grammatical, spelling, punctuation, or usage errors. Make sure that the supporting details are clear and in a logical order in a report. Rework the dialogue to make it more precise in a story. Read your work to someone else and ask for feedback. Finally, revise it again.

Internet Technology

Online sources are a wonderful tool for writers. They can get works published at little or no cost either as an e-book or a printed book. There are other options available as well, such as editing and marketing services offered on many Internet sites. Writing tools give help with everything from style to grammar. Many sites are reliable research possibilities and provide accurate and objective information. Make sure to pick reliable sources for any research. Also, be sure to cite Internet sources using an accepted format such as that from the MLA (Modern Language Association). Many sites allow people to work together on projects regardless of their physical location. Chat rooms and topic websites are other tools that allow exchanges of information and have shared writing projects.

PRESENTING CLAIMS AND COUNTERCLAIMS FAIRLY

When making a claim, it is important to first think about the arguments that support that claim. While researching, try to anticipate what readers might say; this will help you thoroughly develop your claim. It is not enough to research a claim on the Internet, because many sources are dubious at best. Look for sites that are objective. Find authorities that you can quote, and use statistics. Present counterclaims using ample evidence. Mention both the strengths and weaknesses without any prejudice. Divide each counterclaim into a separate paragraph with supporting evidence. Make sure to present everything in a logical manner so that the information will be easily understood by the reader. Most importantly, one needs to separate opinions from facts.

SETTING THE STAGE FOR A NARRATIVE

To set the stage for a narrative, you need to introduce the reader to the setting and the characters. Next, you should introduce a plot line. This should consist of various events that lead to a problem, a climax, and a resolution. This gives a narrative structure. The way in which the author introduces these elements has an influence on the overall effectiveness of the narrative. Make sure to use language to describe the setting and the characters that will grab the reader's attention. Make the details specific. The conclusion or resolution will allow you to tie up the details of the story.

INTRODUCING A NARRATOR

The narrator in a story is the person doing the "speaking," or the one who is telling the story. A narrator can speak in the first or third person. The narrator can shift from one person to another during the course of the story. It is even possible for the narrator to be non-human. The introduction of your narrator can be quick, subtle, dramatic, or humorous; it is up to you. Many times, an event or a circumstance opens the story. Make sure any details about time, place, and circumstance are developed logically and naturally, and that the reader will understand who (or what) the narrator is and where the narrator fits into the story.

F. **Scott Fitzgerald's novel *The Great Gatsby***

Fitzgerald was writing about a time when there was a period of great wealth in the country, as well as great excess and abandon, after the end of World War I. He portrays society's fascination with the ideals of wealth and happiness, the so-called "American Dream." The two main characters, Nick and Gatsby, both of whom served their country during the war, are cynical and disillusioned. Gatsby throws lavish parties at his estate every weekend with liquor (outlawed by the Eighteenth Amendment) flowing freely. Fitzgerald captures the mood with striking clarity, portraying the moral emptiness of the time and the growing distrust of the wealthy as the decade careened towards its close with the Great Depression of 1929.

PURPOSE OF THE FOLLOWING EXCERPT FROM FRANKLIN D. ROOSEVELT'S SPEECH OF JULY 2, 1932

"I pledge you, I pledge myself, to a new deal for the American people. Let us all here assembled constitute ourselves prophets of a new order of competence and of courage. This is more than a political campaign; it is a call to arms..."

In this speech given by Franklin D. Roosevelt when he accepted the Democratic nomination for President, he proposed launching a new effort to turn back the tide of Depression that had gripped the country for several years. In using the phrase "a call to arms," he addressed the audience in a manner similar to how a commander would address his soldiers. His purpose was to contrast himself and the Democratic Party with the Republican view of government, which favored big businesses and a continuation of the policies of Herbert Hoover. He subsequently went on to win in a landslide victory in November, and his policies, of course, went on to be labeled by history as The New Deal.

Run-on Sentence

Run-on sentences are independent clauses that have not been joined correctly. An independent clause is a word group that does or could stand alone in a sentence. When two or more independent clauses appear in one sentence, they must be joined in one of these ways:

1. Revision with a comma and a coordinating conjunction
2. Revision with a semicolon, a colon, or a dash, used when independent clauses are closely related and their relationship is clear without a coordinating conjunction
3. Revision by separating sentences, used when both independent clauses are long or if one is a question and one is not: Separate sentences may be the best option in this case.
4. Revision by restructuring the sentence: For sentence variety, consider restructuring the sentence, perhaps by turning one of the independent clauses into a subordinate phrase or clause.

Usually one of these choices will be an obvious solution to the run-on sentence. The fourth technique above is often the most effective solution but requires the most revision.

First Draft

Drafting is a mysterious art and does not easily lend itself to rules. Generally, the more detailed the formal or informal outline is, the easier is the transition to a first draft. Drafting is a learning process, and planning, organizing, and researching may be ongoing. Drafting is an evaluative process as well, and the whole project will be under scrutiny as the draft develops. The scope may be narrowed or widened, the approach may change, and different conclusions may emerge.

The process itself is shaped by the writer's preferences for atmosphere during the writing process. Time of day or night, physical location, ambient conditions, and any useful rituals can all play into the writer's comfort and productivity. The creation of an atmosphere conducive to the writer's best work is a subtle but important aspect of writing that is often overlooked. Although excellent writing has often been done in difficult situations, it is not the best prescription for success.

Examining Paragraphs and Sentences

Paragraphs are a key structural unit of prose used to break up long stretches of words into more manageable subsets and to indicate a shift in topics or focus. Each paragraph may be examined by identifying the main point of the section and ensuring that every sentence supports or relates to the main theme. Paragraphs may be checked to make sure the organization used in each is appropriate and that the number of sentences is adequate to develop the topic.

Sentences are the building blocks of the written word, and they can be varied by paying attention to sentence length, sentence structure, and sentence openings. These elements should be varied so that writing does not seem boring, repetitive, or choppy. A careful analysis of a piece of writing will expose these stylistic problems, and they can be corrected before the final draft is written. Varying sentence structure and length can make writing more inviting and appealing to a reader.

Editing Process

Time must always be allowed for thorough and careful editing to ensure clean and error-free work. It is helpful to create a checklist of editing to use as the manuscript is proofed. Patterns of editing problems often become apparent, and understanding these patterns can eliminate them. Examples of patterns of errors include misuse of commas, difficulty in shifting tenses, and spelling problems.

Once these patterns are seen, it is much easier to avoid them in the original writing. A checklist should be prepared based on every piece of writing, and it should be cumulative. In this manner, progress may be checked regularly, and the quantity and type of errors should be reduced over time. It is often helpful to have a peer proof a manuscript, to get a fresh set of eyes on the material. Editing should be treated as an opportunity to polish and perfect a written work rather than a chore that must be done. A good editor usually turns into a better writer over time.

Analyzing an Assigned Topic

In academic settings, a teacher assigns many topics. The assignment should be carefully studied with special attention paid to the following elements:

1. Determine the purpose of the assignment. It may be to compare, contrast, describe, or narrate. Key words in the instructions will be a good guide.
2. Identify the audience if it is to include someone besides the teacher. An analysis of the audience and its knowledge and expectations is always helpful.
3. Note the length of the assignment. Does it limit or require a certain number of pages? If so, what are the parameters?
4. It is important to note the deadline for an assignment. Sometimes preliminary materials are to be submitted before the main assignment. Considering these factors will give a writer information needed to set a schedule for the project.

The better an assignment is specifically understood, the more smoothly the writing can unfold. Extra time spent in this understanding is rarely wasted.

Drafting the Research Essay

Before beginning the research essay, revisit the purpose, audience, and scope of the essay. An explicit thesis statement should summarize major arguments and approaches to the subject. After determining the special format of the essay, a survey of the literature on the subject is helpful. If original or first-hand research is involved, prepare a summary of the methods and conclusions.

A clustering strategy assembles all pertinent information on a topic in one physical place. The preparation of an outline may be based on the clusters, or a first draft may be developed without an outline. Formal outlines use a format of thesis statement, main topic, and supporting ideas to shape the information. Drafting the essay can vary considerably among researchers, but it is useful to use an outline or information clusters to get started. Drafts are usually done on a point-to-point basis.

The introduction to a research essay is particularly important, as it sets the context for the essay. It needs to draw the reader into the subject and provide necessary background to understand the subject. It is sometimes helpful to open with the research question and explain how the question will be answered. The major points of the essay may be forecast or previewed to prepare readers for the coming arguments.

In a research essay, it is a good idea to establish the writer's credibility by reviewing credentials and experience with the subject. Another useful opening involves quoting several sources that support the points of the essay, again to establish credibility. The tone should be appropriate to the audience and subject, maintaining a sense of careful authority while building the arguments. Jargon should be kept to a minimum, and language should be carefully chosen to reflect the appropriate tone.

Drafting the Conclusion

The conclusion to a research essay helps readers summarize what they have learned. Conclusions are not meant to convince, as this has been done in the body of the essay. It can be useful to leave the reader with a memorable phrase or example that supports the argument. Conclusions should be both memorable and logical restatements of the arguments in the body of the essay.

A specific-to-general pattern can be helpful, opening with the thesis statement and expanding to more general observations. A good idea is to restate the main points in the body of the essay, leading to the conclusion. An ending that evokes a vivid image or asks a provocative question makes the essay memorable. The same effect can be achieved by a call for action, or a warning. Conclusions may be tailored to the audience's background, in terms of language, tone, and style.

Global Revisions

Global revisions address the larger elements of writing. They usually affect paragraphs or sections, and may involve condensing or merging sections of text to improve meaning and flow. Sometimes material may be rearranged to better present the arguments of the essay. It is usually better for the writer to get some distance from the work before starting a global revision. Reviewers and editors can be usefully employed to make suggestions for revision. If reviewers are used, it is helpful to emphasize the focus on the larger themes of the work rather than the finer points. When undertaking a global review, the writer might wish to position himself or herself as the audience rather than the writer. This provides some additional objectivity and can result in a more honest appraisal of the writing and revisions that should be made. Global revisions are the last major changes a writer will make in the text.

Answering the following questions as objectively as possible will allow for a useful global revision:

1. Purpose: Does the draft accomplish its purpose? Are the material and tone appropriate for the intended audience? Does it account for the audience's knowledge of the subject? Does it seek to persuade, inform, or entertain them?
2. Focus: Does the introduction and the conclusion focus on the main point? Are all supporting arguments focused on the thesis?
3. Organization and paragraphing: Are there enough organizational cues to guide the reader? Are any paragraphs too long or too short?
4. Content: Is the supporting material persuasive? Are all ideas adequately developed? Is there any material that could be deleted?
5. Point of view: Is the draft free of distracting shifts in point of view? Is the point of view appropriate for the subject and intended audience?

Sentence Revision and Editing

Revising sentences is done to make writing more effective. Editing sentences is done to correct any errors. Revising sentences is usually best done on a computer, on which it is possible to try several versions easily. Some writers prefer to print out a hard copy and work with this for revisions. Each works equally well and depends on the individual preference.

Spelling and grammar checks on software are a great aid to a writer, but not a panacea. Many grammatical problems—such as faulty parallelism, mixed constructions, and misplaced modifiers—can slip past the programs. Even if errors are caught, the writing still must be evaluated for effectiveness. A combination of software programs and writer awareness is necessary to ensure an error-free manuscript.

Main Point of a Paragraph

A paragraph should be unified around a main point. A good topic sentence summarizes the paragraph's main point. A topic sentence is more general than subsequent supporting sentences are. Sometime the topic sentence will be used to close the paragraph if earlier sentences give a clear indication of the direction of the paragraph. Sticking to the main point means deleting or omitting unnecessary sentences that do not advance the main point.

The main point of a paragraph deserves adequate development, which usually means a substantial paragraph. A paragraph of two or three sentences often does not develop a point well enough, particularly if the point is a strong supporting argument of the thesis. An occasional short paragraph is fine, particularly if it is used as a transitional device. A choppy appearance should be avoided.

Making Paragraphs Coherent

A smooth flow of sentences and paragraphs without gaps, shifts, or bumps leads to paragraph coherence. Ties between old and new information can be smoothed by several strategies:

1. Linking ideas clearly, from the topic sentence to the body of the paragraph, is essential for a smooth transition. The topic sentence states the main point, and this should be followed by specific details, examples, and illustrations that support the topic sentence. The support may be direct or indirect. In indirect support, the illustrations and examples may support a sentence that in turn supports the topic directly.
2. The repetition of key words adds coherence to a paragraph. To avoid dull language, variations of the key words may be used.
3. Parallel structures are often used within sentences to emphasize the similarity of ideas and connect sentences giving similar information.
4. Maintaining a consistent verb tense throughout the paragraph helps. Shifting tenses affects the smooth flow of words and can disrupt the coherence of the paragraph.

Transitions

Transitions are bridges between what has been read and what is about to be read. Transitions smooth the reader's path between sentences and inform the reader of major connections to new ideas forthcoming in the text. Transitional phrases should be used with care, selecting the appropriate phrase for a transition. Tone is another important consideration in using transitional phrases, varying the tone for different audiences. For example, in a scholarly essay, "in summary" would be preferable to the more informal "in short."

When working with transitional words and phrases, writers usually find a natural flow that indicates when a transition is needed. In reading a draft of the text, it should become apparent where the flow is uneven or rough. At this point, the writer can add transitional elements during the revision process. Revising can also afford an opportunity to delete transitional devices that seem heavy handed or unnecessary.

Argumentative Writing

In constructing a reasonable argument, the goal is not to win or have the last word but rather to reveal current understanding of the question and propose a solution to the perceived problem. The purpose of argument in a free society or a research field is to reach the best conclusion possible at the time.

Conventions of arguments vary from culture to culture. In America, arguments tend to be direct rather than subtle, carefully organized rather than discursive, spoken plainly rather than poetically. Evidence presented is usually specific and factual, and appeals to intuition or communal wisdom are rare.

Argumentative writing takes a stand on a debatable issue and seeks to explore all sides of the issue and reach the best possible solution. Argumentative writing should not be combative; at its strongest, it is assertive.

A prelude to argumentative writing is an examination of the issue's social and intellectual contexts.

Composition and Composition Studies

Composition refers to a range of activities, which includes the achievement of literacy, transmission of culture, preparation for writing skills in the workplace, and writing as a mode of personal expression and identity. Composition has evolved into an interdisciplinary study and an eclectic practice. The process of writing always performs a critical role in education.

Composition studies, like its companion rhetoric, is a practical and theoretical study. Originally it was limited to teaching and correction of students' grammar. Composition has come of age as a writing process, a complex network of interweaving social, political, and individual components.

The field now includes collaborative writing, which is two or more students writing together, each assuming specific responsibilities with a heavy emphasis on joint revisions. Continued innovations and experimentation are an ongoing part of composition studies.

Language Conventions

Spelling, Punctuation and Capitalization

Writing is an extension of who someone is. As the author, that person is in control of the words chosen, the way they are spelled, the sentence structure and variety used, and the presentation of the work. People who do not know the author personally may read the text. Someone may judge the author, as a person, on the quality of their writing. For this reason, crafting a legible work that displays accurate spelling and correct use of grammar is important. Spelling accurately and using the conventions of punctuation and capitalization correctly makes the author seem like the intelligent person they are.

Pronoun-Antecedent Agreement

Pronoun-antecedent agreement means that the pronoun and the antecedent (the word that refers back to the pronoun) need to match in number and gender. A singular pronoun needs a singular antecedent, just as a plural pronoun needs a plural antecedent. Likewise, masculine pronouns need masculine antecedents, and feminine pronouns need feminine antecedents. Here is an example of a sentence with a mistake in pronoun-antecedent agreement: The bike rack is there for everyone to lock up their bikes. This is a very common error and one that people make in speaking and in writing all the time. In the sentence, the pronoun is their. This is a plural pronoun. In the sentence, the antecedent is everyone, which is singular. The sentence should have correct pronoun-antecedent agreement. Here is the correct revision of the sentence:

> The bike rack is there for everyone to lock up his bike.

Prepositions and Conjunctions

A preposition is a word placed before a noun or pronoun to form a phrase modifying another word in the sentence. The prepositional phrase usually functions as an adjective or adverb. There are a limited number of prepositions in English, perhaps around 80. Some prepositions are more than one word long. *Along with, listen to*, and *next to* are some examples.

Conjunctions join words, phrases, or clauses, and they indicate the relationship between the elements that are joined. There are coordinating conjunctions that connect grammatically equal elements, correlative conjunctions that connect pairs, subordinating conjunctions that introduce a subordinate clause, and conjunctive adverbs, which may be used with a semicolon to connect independent clauses. The most common conjunctive adverbs include *then, thus,* and *however*. Using conjunctions correctly helps avoid sentence fragments and run-on sentences.

Verbs

The verb of a sentence usually expresses action or being. It is composed of a main verb and sometimes supporting verbs. These helping verbs are forms of *have, do*, and *be,* and nine modals. The modals are *can, could, may, might, shall, should, will, would*, and *ought*. Some verbs are followed by words that look like prepositions but are so closely associated with the verb as to be part of its meaning. These words are known as particles, and examples include *call off, look up*, and *drop off.*

The main verb of a sentence is always one that would change form from base form to past tense, past participle, present participle, and *–s* forms. When both the past-tense and past-participle forms of a verb end in *–ed,* the verb is regular. In all other cases, the verb is irregular. The verb *to be* is highly irregular, having eight forms instead of the usual five.

Verbal Phrases

A verbal phrase is a verb form that does not function as the verb of a clause. There are three major types of verbal phrases:

1. Participial phrases: These always function as adjectives. Their verbals are always present participles, always ending in *-ing*, or past participles frequently ending in *-d,-ed,-n,-en*, or *-t*. Participial phrases frequently appear immediately following the noun or pronoun they modify.
2. Gerund phrases: Gerund phrases are built around present participles, and they always function as nouns, usually as subjects, subject complements, direct objects, or objects of a preposition.
3. Infinitive phrases are usually structured around *to* plus the base form of the verb. They can function as nouns, as adjectives, or as adverbs. When functioning as a noun, an infinitive phrase may appear in almost any noun slot in a sentence, usually as a subject, subject complement, or direct object. Infinitive phrases functioning as adjectives usually appear immediately following the noun or pronoun they modify. Adverbial phrases usually qualify the meaning of the verb.

Appositive and Absolute Phrases

Strictly speaking, appositive phrases are not subordinate word groups. Appositive phrases function somewhat as adjectives do, to describe nouns or pronouns. Instead of modifying nouns or pronouns, however, appositive phrases rename them. In form, they are nouns or noun equivalents. Appositives are said to be in apposition to the nouns or pronouns they rename. For example, in the sentence "Terriers, hunters at heart, have been dandied up to look like lap dogs," *hunters at heart* is in apposition to the noun *terriers*.

An absolute phrase modifies a whole clause or sentence, not just one word, and it may appear nearly anywhere in the sentence. It consists of a noun or noun equivalent usually followed by a participial phrase. Both appositive and absolute phrases can cause confusion in their usage in grammatical structures. They are particularly difficult for a person whose first language is not English.

Sentence Classification

Sentences are classified in two ways: according to their structure or to their purpose.

Writers use declarative sentences to make statements, imperative sentences to issue requests or commands, interrogative sentences to ask questions, and exclamatory sentences to make exclamations.

Depending on the number and types of clauses they contain, sentences may be classified as simple, compound, complex, or compound-complex.

Clauses come in two varieties: independent and subordinate. An independent clause is a full sentence pattern that does not function within another sentence pattern; it contains a subject and modifiers plus a verb and any objects, complements, and modifiers of that verb, and it either stands alone or could stand alone. A subordinate clause is a full sentence pattern that functions within a sentence as an adjective, an adverb, or a noun but cannot stand alone as a complete sentence.

Sentence Structure

The four major types of sentence structure are:

1. Simple sentences: Simple sentences have one independent clause with no subordinate clauses. A simple sentence may contain compound elements—a compound subject, verb, or object, for example—but does not contain more than one full sentence pattern.
2. Compound sentences: Compound sentences are composed of two or more independent clauses with no subordinate clauses. The independent clauses are usually joined with a comma and a coordinating conjunction or with a semicolon.
3. Complex sentences: A complex sentence is composed of one independent clause with one or more dependent clauses.
4. Compound-complex sentences: A compound-complex sentence contains at least two independent clauses and at least one subordinate clause. Sometimes they contain two full sentence patterns that can stand alone. When each independent clause contains a subordinate clause, this makes the sentence both compound and complex.

Adjective and Adverb

Adjectives modify nouns or pronouns; adverbs modify verbs, adjectives, or other adverbs. Adjectives are often misused in place of adverbs to modify verbs in casual or nonstandard speech. Adverbs usually answer one of these questions: When? Where?, How? Why? How often? To what degree? Many adverbs are formed by adding *–ly* to adjectives. However, not all words ending in *–ly* are adverbs. Some adjectives end in *–ly*, and some adverbs do not. Adjectives ordinarily precede nouns, but they can also function as subject complements following linking verbs. When an adjective functions as a subject complement, it describes the subject. Most adjectives and adverbs have three forms: the positive, the comparative, and the superlative. The comparative should be used to compare two things, the superlative to compare three or more things.

Comma

The comma was invented to help readers. Without it, sentence parts can run together, making meanings unclear. Various rules for comma use include the following:

1. Use a comma before a coordinating conjunction joining independent clauses.
2. Use a comma after an introductory clause or phrase.
3. Use a comma between items in a series.
4. Use a comma between coordinate adjectives not joined with *and*. Do not use a comma between cumulative adjectives.
5. Use commas to set off nonrestrictive elements. Do not use commas to set off restrictive elements.
6. Use commas to set off transitional and parenthetical expressions, absolute phrases, and elements expressing contrast.
7. Use commas to set off nouns of direct address, the words *yes* and *no*, interrogative tags, and interjections.
8. Use commas with dates, addresses, titles, and numbers.
9. Use commas to prevent confusion.
10. Use commas to set off direct quotations.

Situations in Which Commas Are Unnecessary

1. Do not use a comma between compound elements that are not independent clauses.
2. Do not use a comma after a phrase that begins with an inverted sentence.

3. Do not use a comma between the first or after the last item in a series or before the word *although*.
4. Do not use a comma between cumulative adjectives, between an adjective and a noun, or between an adverb and an adjective.
5. Do not use commas to set off restrictive or mildly parenthetical elements or to set off an indirect quotation.
6. Do not use a comma to set off a concluding adverb clause that is essential to the meaning of the sentence or after the word *although*.
7. Do not use a comma to separate a verb from its subject or object. 8. Do not use a comma after a coordinating conjunction or before a parenthesis.
8. Do not use a comma with a question mark or an exclamation point.

Colon

The colon is used primarily to call attention to the words that follow it. In addition, the colon has some other conventional uses:

1. Use a colon after an independent clause to direct attention to a list, an appositive, or a quotation.
2. Use a colon between independent clauses if the second summarizes or explains the first.
3. Use a colon after the salutation in a formal letter, to indicate hours and minutes, to show proportions, between a title and subtitle, and between city and publisher in bibliographic entries.

A colon must be preceded by a full independent clause. Avoid using colons in the following situations:

1. Between a verb and its object or complement
2. Between a preposition and its object
3. After such as, including, or for example

Semicolon

The semicolon is used to connect major sentence elements of equal grammatical rank. Some rules regarding semicolons include the following:

1. Use a semicolon between closely related independent clauses not joined with a coordinating conjunction.
2. Use a semicolon between independent clauses linked with a transitional expression.
3. Use a semicolon between items in a series containing internal punctuation.
4. Avoid using a semicolon between a subordinate clause and the rest of the sentence.
5. Avoid using a semicolon between an appositive word and the word it refers to.
6. Avoid using a semicolon to introduce a list.
7. Avoid using a semicolon between independent clauses joined by *and, but, or, nor, for, so,* or *yet.*

Apostrophe

An apostrophe is used to indicate that a noun is possessive. Possessive nouns usually indicate ownership, as in *Bill's coat* or *the dog's biscuit*. Sometimes ownership is only loosely implied, as in *the dog's coat* or *the forest's trees*. If it is unclear whether a noun is possessive, turning into phrase may clarify it.

If the noun is plural and ends in–*s*, add only an apostrophe. To show joint possession, use –*'s* with the last noun only. To show individual possession, make all nouns possessive.

An apostrophe is often optional in plural numbers, letters, abbreviations, and words mentioned as words. Common errors in using apostrophes include the following:

1. Using an apostrophe with nouns that are not possessive
2. Using an apostrophe in the possessive pronouns *its, whose, his, hers, ours, yours*, and *theirs*

Quotation Marks

Use quotation marks to enclose direct quotations of a person's words, spoken or written. Do not use quotation marks around indirect quotations. An indirect quotation reports someone's ideas without using that person's exact words.

Set off long quotations of prose or poetry by indenting. Use single quotation marks to enclose a quotation within a quotation. Quotation marks should be used around the titles of short works: newspaper and magazine articles, poems, short stories, songs, episodes of television and radio programs, and subdivisions of books or web sites.

Punctuation is used with quotation marks according to convention. Periods and commas are placed inside quotation marks, whereas colons and semicolons are placed outside quotation marks. Question marks and exclamation points are placed either inside or outside quotation marks, depending on the rest of the material in the sentence.

Do not use quotation marks around the title of your own essay.

Dash, Parentheses, and Brackets

Dashes are used for the following purposes:

1. To set off parenthetical material that deserves emphasis
2. To set off appositives that contain commas
3. To prepare for a list, a restatement, an amplification, or a dramatic shift in tone or thought

Unless there is a specific reason for using the dash, omit it. It can give text a choppy effect.

Parentheses are used to enclose supplemental material, minor digressions, and afterthoughts. They are also used to enclose letters or numbers, labeling them items in a series. Parentheses should be used sparingly, as they break up text in a distracting manner when overused.

Brackets are used to enclose any words or phrases that have been inserted into an otherwise word-for-word quotation.

Ellipsis Mark and the Slash

The ellipsis mark consists of three spaced periods (...) and is used to indicate when certain words have been deleted from an otherwise word-for-word quotation. If a full sentence or more is deleted in the middle of a quoted passage, a period should be inserted before the ellipsis dots. The ellipsis mark should not be used at the beginning of a quotation. It should also not be used at the end of a quotation unless some words have been deleted from the end of the final sentence.

The slash (/) may be used to separate two or three lines of poetry that have been run into a text. If there are more than three lines of poetry they should be handled as an indented quotation. The slash may occasionally be used to separate paired terms such as passed/failed or either/or. In this case, a space is not placed before or after the slash. The slash should be used sparingly, only when it is clearly appropriate.

Comma Splice

A comma splice is the use of a comma between two independent clauses. A comma splice can typically be corrected by changing the comma to a period and therefore making the two clauses into two separate sentences, by changing the comma to a semicolon, or by making one clause dependent by inserting a dependent marker word in front of it.

Incorrect: She eats an apple every day, it tastes delicious.

Correct: She eats an apple every day. It tastes delicious.

(or) She eats an apple every day; it tastes delicious.

(or) She eats an apple every day, and it tastes delicious.

(or) She eats an apple every day because it tastes delicious.

(or) Because it tastes delicious, she eats an apple every day.

Adjective

An *adjective* modifies a noun, a pronoun, or another adjective by answering the following questions: What kind of? Which one? How many? How much? Adjectives can appear in three places: before a noun, after a linking or sensory verb (be, feel, look, seem, smell, sound, etc.), and after a direct object as an objective complement.

Examples:

1. The United States is a wonderful place to live. (adjective is before a noun)
2. The baby seems happier after a nap. (adjective follows a linking verb)
3. The military has worked to keep us safe. (the adjective is an objective complement)

Nouns, pronouns, and participles sometimes act as adjectives. Examples:

1. The student government elected a president. noun
2. This is a exciting time. present participle
3. We viewed the demolished building. past participle
4. This china is very old. demonstrative pronoun
5. Which movie did you see? interrogative pronoun
6. His haircut was hideous. possessive pronoun

Equal Comparison Adjectives

Equal comparisons - Use as...as to compare two persons, places, or things which are apparently the same.

Examples:

1. He is as short as I am.
2. Her cat is as fussy as his cat is.
3. Josh's swing is as old and rusty as mine is.
4. That little chair is as expensive as my big sofa.

Unequal comparison adjectives

One-syllable adjectives use -er/est or less/least

Positive: new

Comparative (compares exactly 2 things): newer

Superlative (denotes extreme of 3 or more things): newest

Two-syllable adjectives ending in 'y' use -ier/iest or less/least

Positive: hungry

Comparative: hungrier

Superlative: the hungriest

Other two-or-more syllable adjectives use more/most, less/least before adjective

Positive: thrilling

Comparative: more thrilling

Superlative: the most thrilling

A few adjectives have irregular comparative and superlative forms.

Positive: bad

Comparative: worse

Superlative: worst

Adjective phrases

Adjective phrases are groups of words used as adjectives.

Participial phrases consist of a participle, its object, and any modifiers. Participles show tense and voice.

1. The boy shooting the ball is the team captain.
2. Having finished his homework, Jerry watched TV.
3. The most popular chocolate (being) eaten today is dark chocolate. (passive voice)

Infinitive phrases consist of to+verb, its object, and any modifiers. Infinitives show tense and voice.

1. The play to read for class is Romeo and Juliet.
2. Life is to be enjoyed. passive voice

Prepositional phrases consist of a preposition, its object, and any modifiers.

1. The dog with the spots is a dalmation.
2. The President lives in a mansion in Washington D.C.

ADVERB

An *adverb* modifies a verb, an adjective, or another adverb by answering such questions as how? how much? how long? when? and where? Adverbs also act as sentence modifiers.

1. He dressed handsomely. how?
2. She knows more than she thinks. how much?
3. He was gone a week. how long?
4. Last month they flew to Hawaii. when?
5. I went home. where?
6. Unfortunately, he revealed the story's surprise ending. sentence modifier

Other Parts of Speech as Adverbs - Nouns, prepositions and adjectives sometimes act as adverbs.

1. I'll see you Friday. noun when?
2. He came outside. preposition where?
3. My brother Fred runs slow. adjective how?

Adverbs Formed by Adding 'LY' to Adjectives - An adverb is often formed by adding an 'ly' to an adjective.

ADVERB PHRASES

Adverb phrases are groups of words used as adverbs.

Prepositional phrases consist of a preposition, its object, and any modifiers.

1. Jonah lived in a whale for a month. how long?
2. Jack and Jill walked to the store. where?
3. They got married after leaving town. when?

Infinitive phrases consist of to+verb, any object, and modifiers.

1. My grandfather left home to sail around the world. why?
2. It costs a lot of money to get a good education. clause modifier

Absolute phrases consist of a participle, its subject, and any modifiers. Absolute phrases modify the entire sentence.

The crowd being totally out of control, the police shot off tear gas.

ADVERB EQUAL COMPARISONS

Equal Comparisons - Use as...as to compare two similar actions.

1. Jane cooks as well as her mother does.
2. The faucet drips as slowly as molasses.

3. He never managed as successfully as his brother did.
4. Citizens are treated as well as non-citizens in Albania.

Adverb Unequal Comparisons

Unequal Comparisons - Adverbs can be used to compare and contrast dissimilar actions.

Comparative: to compare two actions, use -er/more, less.

Superlative: to refer to the one in a group of three or more that is the outstanding example of the action, use -est/most, least.

One-syllable adverbs use -er/est or less/least

Positive: late

Comparative: later

Superlative: the latest

Two & more syllables use more/most or less/least

Positive: carefully

Comparative: more carefully

Superlative: the most carefully

Irregular Adverbs

Positive: well

Comparative: better

Superlative: the best

Articles

Articles (a/an/the) come before a noun and provide important information. "A/an" are often identified as indefinite articles while "the" is identified as the definite article.

Use a/an with singular count nouns to introduce a singular count noun or to discuss all members of a category.

Omit the article with plural count nouns and non-count nouns to indicate some, an indefinite amount; to discuss an abstract non-count noun; and to represent all members of a category.

Use "the" with count nouns and non-count nouns to indicate something that has already been mentioned; to indicate that reader and writer know the something which they refer to; to indicate a noun identified by an adjective phrase or adjective clause; to indicate one of a kind; in science, to represent all members of a category.

Independent Clause and a Dependent Clause

An i*ndependent clause* is a group of words that contains a subject and verb and expresses a complete thought. An independent clause can be a complete sentence.

A *dependent clause* is a group of words that contains a subject and verb but does not express a complete thought. A dependent clause cannot be a sentence. Dependent clauses can be a noun clause, adjective clause, or an adverb clause.

A *noun clause* can be a subject, a direct or indirect object, or an object of a preposition. Noun clauses can begin with wh- question words (what, which, when, where, who, whom) and question words like how, if, that.

An *adjective clause* modifies a noun or a pronoun. An adjective clause begins with who, whom, which, that, whose, when, where, why and follows the word it modifies.

An *adverb clause* modifies a verb, an adjective, another adverb, or a sentence. An adverb clause answers the question when? where? why? how? to what degree? and under what condition? An adverb clause begins with a subordinating conjunction, such as after, because, since, unless, etc.

Subordinating Conjunctions

Subordinating conjunctions introduce adverbial clauses. They join a dependent adverb clause to an independent clause.

Cause: as, because, since

Comparison: more than, as...as

Conditional: even if, if, unless

Contrast: although, even though, though

Manner: as, as if, as though

Place: where, wherever

Purpose: in order that, so that

Result: so...that

Time: after, before, since, until, when

Coordinating and Correlative Conjunctions

Conjunctions join words, phrases, and clauses, showing the relationship between them.

The categories of conjunctions are coordinating, correlative, and subordinating. Conjunctive adverbs or transition words are another type of conjunction.

Coordinating conjunctions join grammatically equal words, phrases, or clauses (two pronouns, two prepositional phrases, two independent clauses, etc.) The coordinating conjunctions are and, but, or, nor.

Correlative conjunctions are used in pairs to join two or more words, phrases, or clauses that are grammatically equal.

Examples:

both...and; not only...but also; either...or; whether...or; neither...nor

PARTS OF SPEECH

The sentence is the basic unit of communication in English. Parts of speech--*adjectives, adverbs, articles, conjunctions, nouns, pronouns, prepositions, verbs, and interjections*--identify the words which make up a sentence.

Nouns, verbs, adjectives, and adverbs perform essential functions in a sentence and provide the sentence with its content.

Two other parts of speech--conjunctions and prepositions--connect sentences to each other; and, within a sentence, they connect one part--one idea or action--to another.

Some words function only as one part of speech. However, many words can function as two or more parts of speech.

INFINITIVE, PARTICIPIAL, AND PREPOSITIONAL PHRASES

A *phrase* is a group of related words acting as one word-a noun, adjective, or adverb.

Infinitives are to+verb. An infinitive phrase is an infinitive plus any objects and modifiers. Infinitives can act as nouns, adjectives or adverbs.

Participles are verb+ing or verb+ed. Participial phrases can function as nouns, adjectives or adverbs. A participle in a phrase shows tense and voice.

When a participle has an object or modifiers and acts as a noun, it is a *gerund phrase.* When a participle has an object or modifiers and acts as an adjective, it is a participial phrase. When a participle has a subject and modifies an entire sentence, it is an absolute phrase.

A *prepositional phrase* consists of a preposition, its object and any modifiers. Prepositional phrases can act as adjectives or adverbs.

An *appositive phrase* identifies or defines the word it follows.

NOUN

Nouns name things--persons, places, actions or ideas. Nouns are subjects, direct objects, indirect objects, objects of prepositions, predicate complements and predicate nouns. Nouns also show possession. Most nouns name things that can be counted-one potato, two potatoes, three potatoes. Most count nouns are concrete nouns. They name things that can be touched, seen, smelled, heard, tasted-table, movie, flower, song, candy bar. A/an are used with singular count nouns. "The" is used with both singular and plural count nouns.

Collective count nouns identify groups-family, team, herd, crowd, class. Although these nouns represent a group of individuals, they are understood as one unit and take a singular verb. When they represent two or more groups, they are plural. Most count nouns form the plural by adding "s" Example: toe-toes. Irregular count nouns form the plural in a variety of ways: count nouns ending in "s, sh, x, or z" add "es"; some count nouns change forms; some count nouns stay the same. Non-count nouns name things that can't be counted. Follow these rules. Never add "s" to a non-count noun; always use a singular verb; never use a/an with a non-count noun; never use many with a non-count noun.

Comparing Nouns

To compare two nouns, use similar to or the same as; to contrast them use different from.

Common noun suffixes (-ance, -ant, -ence, -er, -ism, -ist, -ity, -ment, -ness, -tion, -ship) are often added to other parts of speech to form nouns. They are sometimes even added to other nouns to create new nouns. These suffixes cannot be added at random. When in doubt, check a dictionary.

Verb: commune

Noun: community

Adjective: different

Noun: difference

Noun: account

Noun: accountant

Adjectives, gerunds, infinitives, and prepositions sometimes act as nouns.

Noun Phrases

Noun phrases are groups of words which act as nouns.

A *gerund phrase* consists of a participle (verb+ing or verb+ed) and

its modifiers acting as a noun. Gerunds show tense and voice.

1. Fran hates doing her laundry. direct object
2. Having learned to speak Spanish qualified Jennifer as an interpreter. subject

An *infinitive phrase* consists of to+verb and modifiers or object. Infinitives show tense and voice.

1. To have our own children was always our dream. subject
2. To have met President Reagan would have been a thrill. subject
3. His goal is to become a millionaire. predicate noun

Pronouns

A pronoun always refers back to a noun. That noun is the pronoun's antecedent. Example: She bought some (antecedent) furniture yesterday, but (pronoun) it hasn't arrived. Pronoun and antecedent must agree in number and gender.

Example: We were happy when our (antecedent) relatives came. It was great seeing (pronoun) them.

A personal pronoun refers to a person or thing. A personal pronoun can be a subject, an object, or a possessive. Personal pronouns usually change their form depending on if they are used as the subject or object of a sentence.

1st Person: I, we, me, us, mine, ours

2nd Person: you, yours

3rd Person: he, she, it, they, him, her, them, his, hers, theirs

Interrogative pronouns (who, whom, which, what, and whose) ask questions.

Relative pronouns (who, whom, which, that, whose) introduce adjective and noun clauses. The relative pronoun, what, introduces noun clauses only. Within an adjective or noun clause, the relative pronoun can function as a subject, object, or possessive. Relative pronouns of the -ever form (whatever, whichever, whoever, whomever) have an indefinite meaning: they do not refer back to a specific noun.

Prepositions, Prepositional Phrases, and Preposition Idioms

Prepositions are connectors. They connect the words which follow them to the rest of the sentence. The most commonly used prepositions are listed below:

- about above aboard across after against along among against around at before behind below beneath beside besides between beyond by despite down during except for from in inside into like near of off on out outside over past since through throughout to toward under underneath until up upon with within without

A preposition must be followed by a nominal--a noun, pronoun, gerund, noun phrase, or noun clause.

Prepositional phrases act as adjectives or adverbs.

Idiomatic Use of Prepositions - Some adjectives, nouns, and verbs are always followed by the same preposition--for example, afraid of, agree with.

Sentence Function

An English sentence has two parts, the subject and the predicate. The *subject* identifies the topic of the sentence. The *predicate* comments on the topic. The subject must include a noun or a phrase or clause acting as a noun. The predicate must include a verb.

Example: Fred and his wife like to cook.

Subject: Fred and his wife

Predicate: like to cook.

The purpose of a sentence refers to its function. Does the sentence state a fact or an opinion? Does it ask a question? Does it give a command? Does it show excitement?

Declarative – A declarative sentence makes a statement and ends with a period. Example: Animals have their own language. states a fact

Interrogative – An interrogative sentence asks a question and ends with a question mark. Example: Do animals have their own language?

Imperative – An imperative sentence gives a command or makes a request; it ends with a period or an exclamation point. Example: Come with me.

Exclamatory – An exclamatory sentence shows sudden or strong feeling; it ends with an exclamation point. Example: How beautiful she is!

VERBS

Verbs state what happens (such as eat or run) or describe a state of being (such as be or appear). All verbs indicate time (hear, heard, will hear, is, was, will be).

All verbs need a subject identifying who or what is acting or being- I think; I am.

Some verbs also have a direct object (He eats meat).

Verbs have five forms: *base form, past tense, past participle, present participle, infinitive.*

Regular verbs form the past tense and the past participle by adding -ed to the base form of the verb (kick, kicked, kicked; walk, walked, walked).

Irregular verbs form the past tense and past participle in many different ways: buy, bought, bought; see, saw, seen.

TRANSITIVE AND INTRANSITIVE VERBS

Action verbs tell what happens. They are either transitive (buy, kick, see) or intransitive (walk, fall).

A *transitive verb* is an action verb requiring a direct object (noun, pronoun, noun phrase or clause) to complete its meaning. A transitive verb can also have an indirect object or an objective complement. See examples below:

- Mary showed the ring.
- Mary showed his mom the ring.
- The country elected him President.

An *intransitive verb* is an action verb which can not accept a direct object. An intransitive verb is followed by an adverbial modifier-an adverb, a prepositional phrase-or nothing at all. See examples below:

- Fred jumped high.
- Fred jumped in the puddle.
- Fred jumped.

LINKING VERBS

Linking verbs do not express action; linking verbs express a state of being. Linking verbs are followed by nouns or adjectives. Examples: John was a doctor. This grapefruit is too sour.

Here is a list of frequently used linking verbs:

- Be (am, is, are, was, were, being, been) is the most common linking verb. Sense-related verbs (feel, look, smell, sound, taste) also act as linking verbs.

Some other verbs (appear, become, grow, seem) can also act as linking verbs. An adjective following a linking verb describes the subject. Example: This fruit is really mushy.

A noun following a linking verb renames the subject. Example: He is a doctor. An adjective following a linking verb describes the subject. Example: Seth was content.

Some verbs (appear, become, feel, grow, look, smell, sound, and taste) are either linking verbs or action verbs, depending on their meaning in a sentence.

Linking verb: Mary grew ill.

Action verb: We grew tomatoes.

Simple Present, Simple Past, and Future Verb Tenses

Verbs change form to agree with the subject of the action and to indicate the time or tense of the action. Verb tenses can be categorized as simple or perfect. Each of these tenses has a continuous form.

Simple present tense expresses habitual or repeated actions, general truths, future actions, literary or historic present, and states or qualities of being. In statements, do/does expresses emphasis. See examples below:

- Susie exercises on Thursdays and Fridays. habitual action
- Fred is a doctor. linking verb--state of being

Simple past tense expresses finished actions. Did in statements expresses emphasis. See examples below.

- World War II ended in 1945. finished action
- Benedict Arnold began as a loyal American, but later he did betray his country. emphasis

Future tense expresses actions or conditions occurring in the future. Simple present tense with an adverb of time can indicate future.

- She will see it next week. future tense
- The insurance coverage ends next month. simple present

Present Perfect, Past Perfect, and Future Perfect Verb Tenses

The *present perfect* tense emphasizes the completion of an action in the very recent past.

Example:

I have just purchased a necklace.

The *present perfect tense* can also indicate an action begun in the past and continued up to the present moment. See example below:

Sam has lived at the same house for ten years.

The *past perfect* indicates how two finished actions are related in time. The first completed action uses the past perfect while the second action uses the simple past. Example:

Before he went blind, Milton had written Paradise Lost.

Future perfect indicates an action to be finished before a future time. Example:

I will have finished the book before I take the exam.

PRESENT, PAST, AND FUTURE CONTINUOUS VERB TENSES

The *present continuous* expresses ongoing but temporary or future actions. See examples below:

- I am riding a bicycle now. ongoing temporary action
- She is flying to Australia next summer. future action

Past continuous usually expresses an action in progress at the time of another past action.

Example:

Sheila was attending a class when the fire alarm went off.

Future continuous expresses a future action. Example:

She will be driving to Maine next year.

PRESENT, PAST, AND FUTURE PERFECT CONTINUOUS VERB TENSES

The *present perfect continuous* emphasizes that an action which began in the past will continue into the future. Example: Arlene has been studying music for three years; she still has one more year to go.

The *future perfect continuous* indicates an action continuing until some specific time in the future. Example: He will have been attending school for nineteen years by the time he graduates.

The *past perfect continuous* emphasizes that the first action continued right up to the time of the second action. Example: By the year 2050, people will have been living on Mars for a decade or more.

ACTIVE VS. PASSIVE VERBS

In an active voice sentence, the subject is the actor. In a passive voice sentence, the opposite is true: the subject is the receiver or the object of the action.

Examples:

- Active voice: Mary rocked the baby.
- Passive voice: The baby was rocked by Mary.

Only transitive verbs use the passive voice.

The passive voice is formed by using be (am, is, are, was, were, being, been) + past participle.

AUXILIARY VERBS

Auxiliary verbs (helping verbs and modals) convey important information, but they never work alone. They must combine with a main verb.

Helping verbs combine with a main verb to identify verb tense, number and voice and to introduce questions and form negatives. The helping verbs are be, do, have, will.

Be (am/is/are/was/were/been) helps make the continuous forms and the passive voice.

Continuous forms:

be (am/is/are/was/were/been) + present participle + (verb+ing)

Example:

- The girl is running. present continuous
- The girl was running. past continuous
- The girl has been running. present perfect continuous
- The girl had been running. past perfect continuous
- Is the girl running? present continuous
- Was the girl running? past continuous
- Has the girl been running? present perfect continuous
- Had the girl been running? past perfect continuous

Verb Usage in Subjunctive Sentences

The *subjunctive mood* is used in formal written English to express conditions contrary to fact, wishes, requests, or demands. A key to writing accurate subjunctive sentences is to ignore normal rules of tense and number.

'Condition contrary to fact' describes a situation that does not exist now, never existed, and is unlikely ever to exist; for example, if Thomas Jefferson were alive today or if Thomas Jefferson had been alive during the Civil War.

The 'if clause' uses the past tense; the independent clause uses would/could/might and the base form of the verb. Example: If I were a billionaire, I would buy all the TV networks.

The 'if clause' uses past perfect; the independent clause uses a would/could/might and the present perfect tense. Example: If I had been born in 1900, I would have sailed around the world.

Sentences expressing wishes use the subjunctive in the 'that clause.'

For present tense wishes, use were, the simple past tense, or would/could/might and the simple form of the verb in the 'that clause.' Example: I wish that the semester were over now.

When a wish is about the past, use the past perfect or would/could/

might and the present perfect in the 'that clause.' Example:

He wished that the semester had ended before he ran out of money.

Ask, demand, insist, move, recommend, suggest, and urge followed by 'that clauses' use the simple form of the verb to express both present and past tense. Example:

The president asks that everyone work together.

Capitalization Rules

Capitalize the titles of works.

- Capitalize the first and last words and all important words in the titles of *books, magazines, newspapers, poems, stories, plays, and works of art:* **G**one **W**ith the **W**ind (book), **N**ew **Y**ork **T**imes (newspaper).
- Capitalize the *first word of every sentence* (including quoted sentences). Patrick Henry said "**G**ive me liberty or give me death."

- Capitalize the pronoun I.
- Capitalize the *first word in every line of poetry*, whether or not the word begins a sentence. See example below.

For though from out our bourne of Time and Place

The flood may bear me far,

I hope to see my Pilot face to face

When I have crossed the bar.

- Tennyson

Capitalize *titles of persons*.

- Capitalize titles when they are used *before a person's name* as part
- of the name: **P**resident Bush, King David
- Titles following a name or used alone in place of a name are not
- usually capitalized unless used in direct address: the **P**resident of the United States
- Capitalize *family-relationship words* when they are used *before a person's name* and when used *alone in place of the name*: **U**ncle Mike came over for dinner. Hello, **D**ad.

Negation

Negation is the process that turns an affirmative statement (I am the walrus) into its opposite denial (I am not the walrus). Nouns as well as verbs can be grammatically negated, by the use of a negative adjective (There is no walrus), a negative pronoun (Nobody is the walrus), or a negative adverb (I never was the walrus). The negative particles are not and no; the negative particle is placed after the auxiliary verb in a sentence.

In English, negation for most verbs other than be and have, or verb phrases in which be, have or do already occur, requires the recasting of the sentence using the dummy auxiliary verb do, which adds little to the meaning of the negative phrase, but serves as a place to attach the negative particles not, or its contracted form -n't, to:

- I have a walrus.
- I don't have a walrus. (the most common way in contemporary English.)
- I do not see the walrus.
- I am not seeing the walrus.
- I have not seen the walrus.

The verb do also follows this rule, and therefore requires a second instance of itself in order to be marked for negation:

"The walrus doesn't do tricks " not "The walrus doesn't tricks."

Homonyms

Homonyms are words that sound the same and are spelled the same but have different meanings. Some examples of homonyms include stalk (to pursue something) and stalk (the shaft of a plant), bark (the part of a tree) and bark (the noise a dog makes), and bank (the financial institution) and bank (the side of a river).

Homonyms are words that sound the same when spoken but are spelled differently and have different meanings. Mistakes in homonyms signal a carelessness or lack of knowledge on the part of the writer. *There* refers to a location. *Their* is a possessive pronoun. *They're* is a contraction that literally means "they are." Here are the homonyms used correctly in sentences:

- I put my book down over *there* and now it seems to be missing.
- Tommy went over to *their* house after school on Wednesday.
- Where are they? *They're* up front waiting for the band to start playing.

Homonyms are words that sound the same but are spelled differently and have different meanings. It is very important to use the correct word when writing so one needs to know the difference between each word. Mistakes in homonyms signal a carelessness or lack of knowledge on the part of the writer. *To* refers to a location or is part of a verb. *Too* means "a lot" or "also." *Two* is a number. Here are the homonyms used correctly in sentences:

- I walked *to* the corner store and back again.
- "You were at the movie theater? I was there *too*."
- *Two* socks come in a pair.

SYNONYMS

Synonyms are words that share the same or similar meanings. Synonyms can be substitutes for one another while preserving the meaning of a phrase. One word can have several synonyms. Synonyms are a useful tool because they allow one to incorporate variation into their writing or speaking. Instead of using the same word repeatedly, synonyms can be incorporated. Synonyms for the word *many* include *several, a lot, myriad,* and *numerous*. Synonyms for *practical* include *handy, useful,* and *functional*. Synonyms for *walk* include *ambulate, foot, pace,* and *tread*. Synonyms for *happy* include *chipper, lighthearted, sunny, bright,* and *cheery*. Synonyms for *distress* include *concern, trouble,* and *worry*.

Practice Test #1

Practice Questions

QUESTIONS 1 -11 PERTAIN TO THE FOLLOWING PASSAGE:

Pride and Prejudice

By Jane Austen

1. It is a truth universally acknowledged, that a single man in possession of a good fortune, must be in want of a wife.
2. However little known the feelings or views of such a man may be on his first entering a neighbourhood, this truth is so well fixed in the minds of the surrounding families, that he is considered the rightful property of some one or other of their daughters.
3. "My dear Mr. Bennet," said his lady to him one day, "have you heard that Netherfield Park is let at last?"
4. Mr. Bennet replied that he had not.
5. "But it is," returned she; "for Mrs. Long has just been here, and she told me all about it."
6. Mr. Bennet made no answer.
7. "Do you not want to know who has taken it?" cried his wife impatiently.
8. "*You* want to tell me, and I have no objection to hearing it."
9. This was invitation enough.
10. "Why, my dear, you must know, Mrs. Long says that Netherfield is taken by a young man of large fortune from the north of England; that he came down on Monday in a chaise and four to see the place, and was so much delighted with it, that he agreed with Mr. Morris immediately; that he is to take possession before Michaelmas, and some of his servants are to be in the house by the end of next week."
11. "What is his name?"
12. "Bingley."
13. "Is he married or single?"
14. "Oh! Single, my dear, to be sure! A single man of large fortune; four or five thousand a year. What a fine thing for our girls!"
15. "How so? How can it affect them?"
16. "My dear Mr. Bennet," replied his wife, "how can you be so tiresome! You must know that I am thinking of his marrying one of them."
17. "Is that his design in settling here?"
18. "Design! Nonsense, how can you talk so! But it is very likely that he *may* fall in love with one of them, and therefore you must visit him as soon as he comes."
19. "I see no occasion for that. You and the girls may go, or you may send them by themselves, which perhaps will be still better, for as you are as handsome as any of them, Mr. Bingley may like you the best of the party."
20. "My dear, you flatter me. I certainly *have* had my share of beauty, but I do not pretend to be anything extraordinary now. When a woman has five grown-up daughters, she ought to give over thinking of her own beauty."
21. "In such cases, a woman has not often much beauty to think of."
22. "But, my dear, you must indeed go and see Mr. Bingley when he comes into the neighbourhood."
23. "It is more than I engage for, I assure you."

24. "But consider your daughters. Only think what an establishment it would be for one of them. Sir William and Lady Lucas are determined to go, merely on that account, for in general, you know, they visit no newcomers. Indeed you must go, for it will be impossible for *us* to visit him if you do not."
25. "You are over-scrupulous, surely. I dare say Mr. Bingley will be very glad to see you; and I will send a few lines by you to assure him of my hearty consent to his marrying whichever he chooses of the girls; though I must throw in a good word for my little Lizzy."
26. "I desire you will do no such thing. Lizzy is not a bit better than the others; and I am sure she is not half so handsome as Jane, nor half so good-humoured as Lydia. But you are always giving *her* the preference."
27. "They have none of them much to recommend them," replied he; "they are all silly and ignorant like other girls; but Lizzy has something more of quickness than her sisters."
28. "Mr. Bennet, how *can* you abuse your own children in such a way? You take delight in vexing me. You have no compassion for my poor nerves."
29. "You mistake me, my dear. I have a high respect for your nerves. They are my old friends. I have heard you mention them with consideration these last twenty years at least."
30. "Ah, you do not know what I suffer."
31. "But I hope you will get over it, and live to see many young men of four thousand a year come into the neighbourhood."
32. "It will be no use to us, if twenty such should come, since you will not visit them."
33. "Depend upon it, my dear, that when there are twenty, I will visit them all."
34. Mr. Bennet was so odd a mixture of quick parts, sarcastic humour, reserve, and caprice, that the experience of three-and-twenty years had been insufficient to make his wife understand his character. *Her* mind was less difficult to develop. She was a woman of mean understanding, little information, and uncertain temper. When she was discontented, she fancied herself nervous. The business of her life was to get her daughters married; its solace was visiting and news.
35. Chapter 2
36. Mr. Bennet was among the earliest of those who waited on Mr. Bingley. He had always intended to visit him, though to the last always assuring his wife that he should not go; and till the evening after the visit was paid she had no knowledge of it. It was then disclosed in the following manner. Observing his second daughter employed in trimming a hat, he suddenly addressed her with:
37. "I hope Mr. Bingley will like it, Lizzy."
38. "We are not in a way to know *what* Mr. Bingley likes," said her mother resentfully, "since we are not to visit."
39. "But you forget, mamma," said Elizabeth, "that we shall meet him at the assemblies, and that Mrs. Long promised to introduce him."
40. "I do not believe Mrs. Long will do any such thing. She has two nieces of her own. She is a selfish, hypocritical woman, and I have no opinion of her."
41. "No more have I," said Mr. Bennet; "and I am glad to find that you do not depend on her serving you."
42. Mrs. Bennet deigned not to make any reply, but, unable to contain herself, began scolding one of her daughters.
43. "Don't keep coughing so, Kitty, for Heaven's sake! Have a little compassion on my nerves. You tear them to pieces."
44. "Kitty has no discretion in her coughs," said her father; "she times them ill."
45. "I do not cough for my own amusement," replied Kitty fretfully. "When is your next ball to be, Lizzy?"
46. "To-morrow fortnight."

47. "Aye, so it is," cried her mother, "and Mrs. Long does not come back till the day before; so it will be impossible for her to introduce him, for she will not know him herself."
48. "Then, my dear, you may have the advantage of your friend, and introduce Mr. Bingley to *her*."
49. "Impossible, Mr. Bennet, impossible, when I am not acquainted with him myself; how can you be so teasing?"
50. "I honour your circumspection. A fortnight's acquaintance is certainly very little. One cannot know what a man really is by the end of a fortnight. But if *we* do not venture somebody else will; and after all, Mrs. Long and her daughters must stand their chance; and, therefore, as she will think it an act of kindness, if you decline the office, I will take it on myself."
51. The girls stared at their father. Mrs. Bennet said only, "Nonsense, nonsense!"
52. "What can be the meaning of that emphatic exclamation?" cried he. "Do you consider the forms of introduction, and the stress that is laid on them, as nonsense? I cannot quite agree with you *there*. What say you, Mary? For you are a young lady of deep reflection, I know, and read great books and make extracts."
53. Mary wished to say something sensible, but knew not how.
54. "While Mary is adjusting her ideas," he continued, "let us return to Mr. Bingley."
55. "I am sick of Mr. Bingley," cried his wife.
56. "I am sorry to hear *that*; but why did not you tell me that before? If I had known as much this morning I certainly would not have called on him. It is very unlucky; but as I have actually paid the visit, we cannot escape the acquaintance now."
57. The astonishment of the ladies was just what he wished; that of Mrs. Bennet perhaps surpassing the rest; though, when the first tumult of joy was over, she began to declare that it was what she had expected all the while.
58. "How good it was in you, my dear Mr. Bennet! But I knew I should persuade you at last. I was sure you loved your girls too well to neglect such an acquaintance. Well, how pleased I am! and it is such a good joke, too, that you should have gone this morning and never said a word about it till now."
59. "Now, Kitty, you may cough as much as you choose," said Mr. Bennet; and, as he spoke, he left the room, fatigued with the raptures of his wife.
60. "What an excellent father you have, girls!" said she, when the door was shut. "I do not know how you will ever make him amends for his kindness; or me, either, for that matter. At our time of life it is not so pleasant, I can tell you, to be making new acquaintances every day; but for your sakes, we would do anything. Lydia, my love, though you *are* the youngest, I dare say Mr. Bingley will dance with you at the next ball."
61. "Oh!" said Lydia stoutly, "I am not afraid; for though I *am* the youngest, I'm the tallest."
62. The rest of the evening was spent in conjecturing how soon he would return Mr. Bennet's visit, and determining when they should ask him to dinner.

1. Paragraphs 22-24 are mainly about...

a. Introducing the Bennet girls to Mr. Bingley
b. Recent wedding engagements in the neighborhood
c. Sir William and Lady Lucas
d. Convincing Mr. Bennet to visit Mr. Bingley

2. Which plot summary best describes the story?

a. Mr. and Mrs. Bennet are discussing their daughters when they discover that Mr. Bingley is moving to the neighborhood. They go to Netherfield Park to meet him and discover that he is looking for a wife. Mrs. Bennet then introduces Mr. Bingley to her four daughters, and she and her husband talk about whom Mr. Bingley will dance with first at the upcoming ball.
b. Mr. and Mrs. Bennet are having an argument over whether or not Mr. Bennet should visit Mr. Bingley. Mr. Bennet finally agrees to the visit and goes to Netherfield Park. After the visit, he takes Mrs. Bennet and his daughters to Netherfield Park so they can meet Mr. Bingley themselves.
c. Mrs. Bennet tells Mr. Bennet that Mr. Bingley is moving to Netherfield Park and that she hopes he will marry one of their daughters. She asks Mr. Bennet to visit Mr. Bingley so that she and her daughters can be introduced later. Mr. Bennet refuses to visit but later surprises his family by going to Netherfield Park and meeting Mr. Bingley.
d. Mrs. Bennet tells Mr. Bennet that Mr. Bingley is throwing a ball and that she hopes her daughters will be invited to it. She asks Mr. Bennet to go to Netherfield Park to convince Mr. Bingley to invite them, but he refuses. Later, he surprises Mrs. Bennet by getting the invitations from Mr. Bingley. Then, Mrs. Bennet and the girls talk about whom Mr. Bingley will dance with first at the ball.

3. Read the following dictionary entry:

Design [dih-zahyn] noun 1) a sketch or a plan of a work of art or structure 2) a goal, purpose, or intention 3) a treacherous plot 4) the organization of a work of art

Which definition best matches the use of the word *design* in paragraphs 17 and 18?

a. Definition 1
b. Definition 2
c. Definition 3
d. Definition 4

4. What goal of Mrs. Bennet's most drives the story?

a. She wants to meet Mr. Bingley
b. She wants one of her four daughters to marry Mr. Bingley
c. She wants Lydia to have the first dance with Mr. Bingley at the ball
d. She wants Mr. Bennet to go with her to Netherfield Park to meet Mr. Bingley

5. Which sentence best shows Mr. Bennet's sense of humor?

a. Mr. Bennet made no answer.
b. My dear Mr. Bennet, how can you be so tiresome?
c. I have a high respect for your nerves.
d. Mr. Bennet was so odd a mixture of quick parts, sarcastic humour, reserve, and caprice, that the experience of three-and-twenty years had been insufficient to make his wife understand his character.

6. What two things do Mrs. Bennet most take comfort in?

a. Hearing gossip and visiting with friends and acquaintances
b. Hearing news and planning her daughters' marriages
c. Spending time with her daughters
d. Visiting neighbors such as Mr. Bingley

7. Mrs. Bennet feels that she cannot meet Mr. Bingley until her husband has already done so. What does this say about the story's setting?

a. It is set in the current year but takes place in a country other than the United States.
b. It is set in a castle with very strict customs.
c. It is set during an era with strict social rules.
d. It is set in the home of a modern family.

8. From the reactions of Mrs. Bennet in paragraphs 55-60, the reader can conclude that...

a. Mrs. Bennet does not want to hear about Mr. Bingley any more.
b. Mrs. Bennet did not want to hear about Mr. Bingley but changed her mind after she found out that Mr. Bennet had visited him.
c. Mrs. Bennet is starting to feel ill when she talks about Mr. Bingley.
d. Mrs. Bennet is angry with Mr. Bennet for refusing to visit Mr. Bingley.

9. What is Mrs. Bennet's opinion of Mrs. Long?

a. She doesn't have an opinion.
b. She thinks that Mrs. Long is not honest.
c. She thinks that Mrs. Long used to be selfish but is now generous.
d. She believes that Mrs. Long only thinks of herself and is not always honest.

10. In paragraph 1, the phrase "truth universally acknowledged" means...

a. An opinion that some people share.
b. A goal that Mrs. Bennet has.
c. A fact that Mr. and Mrs. Bennet believe in.
d. A fact that most people accept.

11. The author's purpose in paragraph 34 is to...

a. Show why Mrs. Bennet wants her husband to visit Mr. Bingley and why Mr. Bennet refuses to do so.
b. Explain Mr. and Mrs. Bennets' personalities.
c. Show Mr. and Mrs. Bennets' personalities through dialogue.
d. Explain the reason why Mrs. Bennet wants one of her daughters to marry Mr. Bingley.

QUESTIONS 12 -22 PERTAIN TO THE FOLLOWING PASSAGE:

The Story of My Life

By Helen Keller

THE most important day I remember in all my life is the one on which my teacher, Anne Mansfield Sullivan, came to me. I am filled with wonder when I consider the immeasurable contrasts between the two lives which it connects. It was the third of March, 1887, three months before I was seven years old.

On the afternoon of that eventful day, I stood on the porch, dumb, expectant. I guessed vaguely from my mother's signs and from the hurrying to and fro in the house that something unusual was about to happen, so I went to the door and waited on the steps. The afternoon sun penetrated the mass of honeysuckle that covered the porch, and fell on my upturned face. My fingers lingered almost unconsciously on the familiar leaves and blossoms which had just come forth to greet the sweet southern spring. I did not know what the future held of marvel or surprise for me. Anger and bitterness had preyed upon me continually for weeks and a deep languor had succeeded this passionate struggle.

Have you ever been at sea in a dense fog, when it seemed as if a tangible white darkness shut you in, and the great ship, tense and anxious, groped her way toward the shore with plummet and sounding-line, and you waited with beating heart for something to happen? I was like that ship before my education began, only I was without compass or sounding-line, and had no way of knowing how near the harbour was. "Light! give me light!" was the wordless cry of my soul, and the light of love shone on me in that very hour.

I felt approaching footsteps. I stretched out my hand as I supposed to my mother. Some one took it, and I was caught up and held close in the arms of her who had come to reveal all things to me, and, more than all things else, to love me.

The morning after my teacher came she led me into her room and gave me a doll. The little blind children at the Perkins Institution had sent it and Laura Bridgman had dressed it; but I did not know this until afterward. When I had played with it a little while, Miss Sullivan slowly spelled into my hand the word "d-o-l-l." I was at once interested in this finger play and tried to imitate it. When I finally succeeded in making the letters correctly I was flushed with childish pleasure and pride. Running downstairs to my mother I held up my hand and made the letters for doll. I did not know that I was spelling a word or even that words existed; I was simply making my fingers go in monkey-like imitation. In the days that followed I learned to spell in this uncomprehending way a great many words, among them *pin, hat, cup* and a few verbs like *sit, stand* and *walk.* But my teacher had been with me several weeks before I understood that everything has a name.

One day, while I was playing with my new doll, Miss Sullivan put my big rag doll into my lap also, spelled "d-o-l-l" and tried to make me understand that "d-o-l-l" applied to both. Earlier in the day we had had a tussle over the words "m-u-g" and "w-a-t-e-r." Miss Sullivan had tried to impress it upon me that "m-u-g" is *mug* and that "w-a-t-e-r" is *water*, but I persisted in confounding the two. In despair she had dropped the subject for the time, only to renew it at the first opportunity. I became impatient at her repeated attempts and, seizing the new doll, I dashed it upon the floor. I was keenly delighted when I felt the fragments of the broken doll at my feet. Neither sorrow nor regret followed my passionate outburst. I had not loved the doll. In the still, dark world in which I lived there was no strong sentiment of tenderness. I felt my teacher sweep the fragments to one side of the hearth, and I had a sense of satisfaction that the cause of my discomfort was removed. She brought me my hat, and I knew I was going out into the warm sunshine. This thought, if a wordless sensation may be called a thought, made me hop and skip with pleasure.

We walked down the path to the well-house, attracted by the fragrance of the honeysuckle with which it was covered. Some one was drawing water and my teacher placed my hand under the spout. As the cool stream gushed over one hand she spelled into the other the word water, first slowly, then rapidly. I stood still, my whole attention fixed upon the motions of her fingers. Suddenly I felt a misty consciousness as of something forgotten–a thrill of returning thought; and somehow the mystery of language was revealed to me. I knew then that "w-a-t-e-r" meant the wonderful cool something that was flowing over my hand. That living word awakened my soul, gave it light, hope, joy, set it free! There were barriers still, it is true, but barriers that could in time be swept away.

I left the well-house eager to learn. Everything had a name, and each name gave birth to a new thought. As we returned to the house every object which I touched seemed to quiver with life. That was because I saw everything with the strange, new sight that had come to me. On entering the door I remembered the doll I had broken. I felt my way to the hearth and picked up the pieces. I tried vainly to put them together. Then my eyes filled with tears; for I realized what I had done, and for the first time I felt repentance and sorrow.

I learned a great many new words that day. I do not remember what they all were; but I do know that *mother, father, sister, teacher* were among them–words that were to make the world blossom for me, "like Aaron's rod, with flowers." It would have been difficult to find a happier child than I was as I lay in my crib at the close of the eventful day and lived over the joys it had brought me, and for the first time longed for a new day to come.

I RECALL many incidents of the summer of 1887 that followed my soul's sudden awakening. I did nothing but explore with my hands and learn the name of every object that I touched; and the more I handled things and learned their names and uses, the more joyous and confident grew my sense of kinship with the rest of the world.

When the time of daisies and buttercups came Miss Sullivan took me by the hand across the fields, where men were preparing the earth for the seed, to the banks of the Tennessee River, and there, sitting on the warm grass, I had my first lessons in the beneficence of nature. I learned how the sun and the rain make to grow out of the ground every tree that is pleasant to the sight and good for food, how birds build their nests and live and thrive from land to land, how the squirrel, the deer, the lion and every other creature finds food and shelter. As my knowledge of things grew I felt more and more the delight of the world I was in. Long before I learned to do a sum in arithmetic or describe the shape of the earth, Miss Sullivan had taught me to find beauty in the fragrant woods, in every blade of grass, and in the curves and dimples of my baby sister's hand. She linked my earliest thoughts with nature, and made me feel that "birds and flowers and I were happy peers."

But about this time I had an experience which taught me that nature is not always kind. One day my teacher and I were returning from a long ramble. The morning had been fine, but it was growing warm and sultry when at last we turned our faces homeward. Two or three times we stopped to rest under a tree by the wayside. Our last halt was under a wild cherry tree a short distance from the house. The shade was grateful, and the tree was so easy to climb that with my teacher's assistance I was able to scramble to a seat in the branches. It was so cool up in the tree that Miss Sullivan proposed that we have our luncheon there. I promised to keep still while she went to the house to fetch it.

Suddenly a change passed over the tree. All the sun's warmth left the air. I knew the sky was black, because all the heat, which meant light to me, had died out of the atmosphere. A strange odour came up from the earth. I knew it, it was the odour that always precedes a thunderstorm, and a nameless fear clutched at my heart. I felt absolutely alone, cut off from my friends and the firm earth. The immense, the unknown, enfolded me. I remained still and expectant; a chilling terror crept over me. I longed for my teacher's return; but above all things I wanted to get down from that tree.

There was a moment of sinister silence, then a multitudinous stirring of the leaves. A shiver ran through the tree, and the wind sent forth a blast that would have knocked me off had I not clung to the branch with might and main. The tree swayed and strained. The small twigs snapped and fell about me in showers. A wild impulse to jump seized me, but terror held me fast. I crouched down in the fork of the tree. The branches lashed about me. I felt the intermittent jarring that came now and then, as if something heavy had fallen and the shock had traveled up till it reached the limb I sat on. It worked my suspense up to the highest point, and just as I was thinking the tree and I should fall together, my teacher seized my hand and helped me down. I clung to her, trembling with joy to feel the earth under my feet once more. I had learned a new lesson–that nature "wages open war against her children, and under softest touch hides treacherous claws."

12. In paragraph 11, the word *beneficence* means...

a. Kindness
b. Generosity
c. Stinginess
d. Danger

13. Paragraphs 6 and 7 are mainly about the narrator...

a. Learning to write words with a pencil
b. Learning the difference between a mug and water
c. Learning that she can have a temper tantrum to get what she wants
d. Learning that words have meaning

14. Why did Helen hold out her hand in paragraph 4?

a. She thought the visitor was her mother
b. She wanted to greet the visitor
c. She wanted to please her mother
d. She loved the approaching person

15. In paragraphs 13 and 14, Helen felt nervous because...

a. She was lost
b. She was alone
c. It was raining
d. It was windy

16. Which sentence best explains what Helen learned from Miss Sullivan?

a. I learned a great many new words that day
b. There were barriers still, it is true, but barriers that could in time be swept away
c. Everything had a name, and each name gave birth to a new thought
d. It would have been difficult to find a happier child than I was as I lay in my crib at the close of the eventful day and lived over the joys it had brought me, and for the first time longed for a new day to come

17. Which aspect of the selection best shows the close bond between Helen and Miss Sullivan?

a. The moment when Miss Sullivan spells "d-o-l-l" into Helen's hand
b. When Helen cried in paragraph 8
c. When Miss Sullivan proposed eating lunch by the cherry tree
d. The moment when Miss Sullivan pulled Helen from the tree

18. What is a major theme of the passage?

a. Family ties
b. Discovery
c. Disappointment
d. Youth

19. In paragraph 14, the narrator uses the phrase "hides treacherous claws" to explain that...

a. Miss Sullivan, beneath her kind exterior, is very mean
b. Helen continues to have violent temper tantrums
c. Climbing trees can be very dangerous.
d. Nature can be cruel.

20. By telling the story in the order that events occur, the author helps the reader understand...

a. The change that Helen underwent after meeting Miss Sullivan
b. The way in which Helen learned to control her temper tantrums
c. The strategies Miss Sullivan used to control Helen
d. The confusion that Helen felt when she was with Miss Sullivan

21. Based on the passage, the reader can conclude that Helen...

a. Disliked Miss Sullivan
b. Is scared of nature
c. Didn't understand words before Miss Sullivan arrived
d. Never learned how to read or write

22. Which phrase or sentence best shows Helen's state of being before Miss Sullivan's arrival?

a. Have you ever been at sea in a dense fog, when it seemed as if a tangible white darkness shut you in...
b. I did not know what the future held of marvel or surprise for me.
c. I guess vaguely from my mother's signs and from the hurrying to and fro in the house that something unusual was about to happen...
d. The morning after my teacher came she led me into her room and gave me a doll.

USE "PRIDE AND PREJUDICE" AND "THE STORY OF MY LIFE" TO ANSWER QUESTIONS 23-25:

23. What do Helen, the narrator of "The Story of My Life," and Mrs. Bennet from "Pride and Prejudice" have in common?

a. They are not interested in having others understand them
b. They both want something they can't have
c. They get frustrated when others don't do what they want
d. They are looking forward to big changes

24. What theme do both passages share?

a. Learning
b. Hope
c. Good vs. evil
d. Despair

25. What does the relationship between Mr. and Mrs. Bennet in "Pride and Prejudice" have in common with the relationship between Helen and Miss Sullivan in "The Story of My Life"?

a. Constant bickering
b. Joyful discovery
c. Grudging respect
d. Deep care

QUESTIONS 26 – 28 PERTAIN TO THE FOLLOWING VISUAL REPRESENTATION:

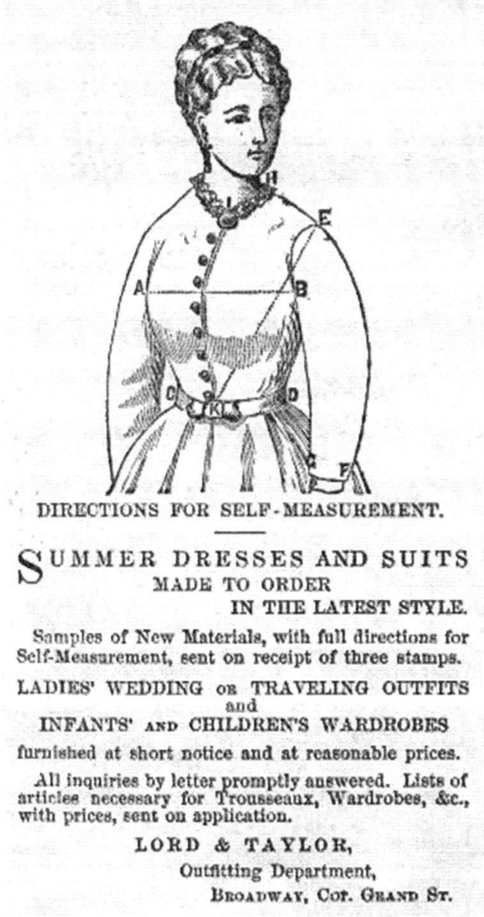

26. Based on the context of the advertisement, what does *receipt* mean?

a. A proof of purchase
b. A piece of paper
c. Instructions for cooking a dish
d. Receive

27. Why does the advertisement give directions for self-measurement?

a. So that the reader can pick out a dress style
b. So that the reader can determine his or her dress size
c. So that the reader can measure the correct lengths of cloth
d. So that the reader can sew the clothes his or herself

28. What does the advertisement mean when it says, "Lists of articles necessary for Trousseaux, Wardrobes, &c., with prices, sent on application"?

a. To convince readers to buy additional items
b. To show that the store also makes clothes for infants and children
c. To prove that all letters are answered
d. To describe the lists of materials that are available

SHORT ANSWER QUESTIONS

29. In "Pride and Prejudice," what kind of relationship do you think Mr. and Mrs. Bennet share? Explain your answer, supporting it with evidence from the selection.

30. In "The Story of My Life," what effect do you think Miss Sullivan had on Helen's life? Explain your answer and support it with evidence from the selection.

31. Who do you think has a closer relationship, Mr. and Mrs. Bennet from "Pride and Prejudice" or Helen and Miss Sullivan in "The Story of My Life"? Explain your answer and support it with evidence from both selections.

REVISING AND EDITING TEXT 1

Johnna's American history teacher has assigned a research essay on a figure from the American Revolution. Johnna decided to write about Paul Revere and would like your help revising and improving the essay. After you read her essay, answer the questions that follow.

> (1) In the early 1760s, Paul Revere, ran a busy metalworking shop. (2) People from all over Boston came to buy the silver and gold cups, medals, and cutlery he made. (3) Everything changed in 1765. (4) Many colonists ran low on money and stopped shopping at Paul's shop.
>
> (5) Things got worse when the british passed the Stamp Act. (6) The Stamp Act created a tax to help the British earn money. (7) Colonists like Paul Revere hated the Stamp Act because it would make things more expensive.
>
> (8) Under the Stamp Act, colonists needed to pay for everything that was printed, such as newspapers, magazines, and business contracts. (9) After a colonist paid the tax, the tax collector put a stamp on the paper to show that the tax had been paid. (10) The Stamp Act made it very expensive for Paul to run his business. (11) For example, if he wanted a new apprentice for his silver shop, he needed to buy a Stamp for the signed contract.
>
> (12) Paul wasn't just angry about buying stamps. (13) He also felt that the British shouldn't be allowed to tax the colonies. (14) There was no American colonists in the British parliament, which passed the tax. (15) Paul and the other colonists didn't want taxation without representation. (16) They wanted to be able to choose their own taxes.
>
> (17) The colonists refused to buy stamps. (18) They were determined to get the Stamp Act repealed.
>
> (19) Paul joined a group called the Sons of Liberty. (20) They wore silver medals on their coats that said "Sons of Liberty." (21) Paul may have helped make the medals in his silver shop.
>
> (22) The Sons of Liberty staged demonstrations at the Liberty Tree, a huge elm tree, that stood in Boston. (23) Paul drew cartoons and wrote poems about liberty. (24) He published them in the local newspaper, *The Boston Gazette*.
>
> (25) After a year of hard work fighting the Stamp Act Paul and the Sons of Liberty received the happy news. (26) The Stamp Act had been repealed!

(27) People celebrated all over Boston; they lit bonfires, set off fireworks, and decorated houses and ships with flags and streamers. (28) Paul attended the biggest celebration, which took place at the Liberty Tree. (29) The people hung 280 lanterns on the tree's branches lighting up the night sky.

(30) Some members of the Sons of Liberty constructed a paper obelisk. (31) An obelisk is the same shape as the Washington Monument. (32) They decorated the obelisk with pictures and verses about the struggle to repeal the Stamp Act and hung it from the Liberty Tree.

(33) Paul may have helped construct the obelisk, even if he wasn't involved in the direct construction, he probably knew about and supported it. (34) After the celebration, he made a copper engraving showing the pictures and verses on the obelisk's four sides. (35) His engraving records the celebration under the Liberty Tree. (36) Even though Paul Revere may be better known for his silver work and famous ride, his engravings, like the engraving of the obelisk, help us see the American Revolution through his eyes.

32. What change should be made to sentence 1?

a. Change *1760s* to *1760's*.
b. Delete the comma after *1760s*.
c. Delete the comma after *Revere*.
d. Add a comma after *busy*.

33. What change should be made to sentence 5?

a. Change *got* to *get*.
b. Change *worse* to *worst*.
c. Change *british* to *British*.
d. Change *Stamp Act* to *stamp act*.

34. What change should be made to sentence 11?

a. Delete the comma after *example*.
b. Delete the comma after *shop*.
c. Change *Stamp* to *stamp*.
d. Change *signed contract* to *Signed Contract*.

35. What change should be made to sentence 14?

a. Change *was* to *were*.
b. Change *parliament* to *parlament*.
c. Delete the comma after *parliament*.
d. Change *which* to *that*.

36. What is the most effective way to combine sentences 17 and 18?

a. The colonists refused to buy stamps and they were determined to get the Stamp Act repealed.
b. The colonists refused to buy stamps, and they were determined to get the Stamp Act repealed.
c. The colonists refused to buy stamps, and were determined to get the Stamp Act repealed.
d. The colonists refused to buy stamps, were determined to get the Stamp Act repealed.

37. What change should be made to sentence 22?

a. Change *demonstrations* to *demonstration*
b. Insert *and* after the comma
c. Delete the comma after *elm tree*
d. Change *in* to *at*

38. What change, if any, should be made to sentence 25?

a. Add a comma after *work*
b. Add a comma after *Act*
c. Change *received* to *recieved*
d. No change

39. What change should be made to sentence 29?

a. Change *280* to *two-hundred-eighty*
b. Change *tree's* to *trees*
c. Add a comma after *branches*
d. Change *night* to *nightly*

40. What is the most effective way to combine sentences 30 and 31?

a. Some members of the Sons of Liberty constructed a paper obelisk, which is the same shape as the Washington Monument.
b. Some members of the Sons of Liberty constructed a paper obelisk which is the same shape as the Washington Monument.
c. Some members of the Sons of Liberty constructed a paper obelisk, that is the same shape as the Washington Monument.
d. Some members of the Sons of Liberty constructed a paper obelisk; which is the same shape as the Washington Monument.

41. What change should be made to sentence 33?

a. Delete *may*
b. Change the comma after *obelisk* to a semicolon
c. Delete the comma after *construction*
d. Change *knew* to *knows*

Revising and Editing Text 2

Landon's German teacher has assigned a research project on the culture and history of Germany. Landon has made a poster and written detailed captions for each set of pictures on the poster. He would like your help revising and improving the captions. After you read Landon's essay, answer the questions that follow.

Berlin

(1) For almost 30 years, the Berlin Wall divided Berlin in two. (2) On November 9, 1989, citizens from both sides of the city joined together to break down the wall and reunite the city. (3) Today, most of the wall has fallen, but a line of bricks snake across the city, marking its old path.

(4) Although bombing during World War II destroyed most of Berlins buildings, the city has been rebuilt as a cultural center. (5) It has art, history, and science museums, as well as famous historical monuments.

(6) The majestic Brandenburg Gate was built in 1791 as a symbols of peace. (7) For many years, it was part of the Berlin Wall and reminded people of the divisions between east and west. (8) Today, the Brandenburg Gate symbolizes reunification and freedom. (9) Near the Brandenburg Gate is the German parliament building, called the Reichstag. (10) It was built in 1894 and was at the center of many important events in German politics. (11) Today, visitors can take an elevator up to the sparkling glass dome at the top of the Reichstag for a view of the city.

Ich bin ein Berliner

(12) On June 26, 1963, President John F. Kennedy visited West Berlin. (13) His visit took place a few years after the Berlin Wall was built and tensions between the United States and Communist East Germany were running high. (14) He gave an inspiring speech about freedom and democracy to the people of democratic West Berlin that ended with words of unity: "Ich bin ein Berliner." (15) He meant to say, "I am a citizen of Berlin," but his words really meant, "I am a doughnut." (16) A Berliner is a jelly doughnut popular in Germany. (17) The Germans in the audience appreciated President Kennedy's support, and cheered his message of freedom enthusiastically.

Cuisine

(18) German cuisine is known for its hearty meat and potato dishes. (19) Families often enjoy a rich Sunday dinner of roast meat, potatoes, and cabbage. (20) A typical Sunday dinner might feature juicy Rinderrouladen, creamy Kartoffelpuree, and sweet Apfelkuchen. (21) In English, that would be stuffed beef rolls, mashed potatoes, and apple cake.

(22) Germans eat their heaviest meal of the day at lunchtime. (23) School cafeterias usually serve hearty stews and side dishes. (24) For dinner, families often eat thin slices of whole wheat bread with sausage, sliced meat, and cheese.

(25) Many Germans enjoy late afternoon Kaffee. (26) They visit a neighborhood café and relax with a cup of coffee and slice of creamy, rich cake. (27) Bakeries dot the streets of German towns and cities, selling from small sandwiches to rich pastries. (28) The Amerikaner cookie, a bakery favorite, is a cakey sugar cookie topped with a vanilla and chocolate glaze. (29) The Americaner got its name because it looks like New York City's famous black and white cookies.

42. What could be deleted from sentence 2 without changing the meaning?

a. 1989
b. from both sides of the city
c. together
d. break down

43. What change should be made to sentence 4?

a. Change *Although* to *However*
b. Add a comma after *World War II*
c. Change *Berlins* to *Berlin's*
d. Change *has* to *had*

44. What change should be made to sentence 6?

a. Change *Gate* to *gate*
b. Change *was* to *were*
c. Insert a comma after *1791*
d. Change *symbols* to *symbol*

45. What change should be made to sentence 13?

a. Change *years* to *year's*
b. Add a comma after *built*
c. Add a comma after *States*
d. Change *were* to *was*

46. What change should be made to sentence 17?

a. Insert commas after *Germans* and *audience*
b. Change *appreciated* to *apreciated*
c. Delete the comma after *support*
d. Change *enthusiastically* to *enthusiaticaly*

47. What change should be made to sentence 18?

a. Change *German* to *Germany*
b. Change *is known* to *knew*
c. Change *its* to *it's*
d. Delete the comma after *hearty*

48. What is the most effective way to combine sentences 18 and 19?

a. German cuisine is known for its hearty meat and potato dishes but families often enjoy a rich Sunday dinner of roast meat, potatoes, and cabbage.
b. German cuisine is known for its hearty meat and potato dishes, but families often enjoy a rich Sunday dinner of roast meat, potatoes, and cabbage.
c. German cuisine is known for its hearty meat and potato dishes, and families often enjoy a rich Sunday dinner of roast meat, potatoes and cabbage.
d. German cuisine is known for its hearty meat and potato dishes, and families often enjoy a rich Sunday dinner of roast meat, potatoes, and cabbage.

49. What is the most concise way to combine sentences 20 and 21 without confusing the reader?

a. A typical Sunday dinner might feature juicy Rinderrouladen, which are stuffed beef rolls, creamy Kartoffelpuree, which are mashed potatoes, and sweet Apfelkuchen, which is apple cake.
b. A typical Sunday dinner might feature juicy Rinderrouladen (stuffed beef rolls), creamy Kartoffelpuree (mashed potatoes), and sweet Apfelkuchen (apple cake).
c. A typical Sunday dinner might feature juicy Rinderrouladen, creamy Kartoffelpuree, and sweet Apfelkuchen, and these are stuffed beef rolls, mashed potatoes, and apple cake.
d. A typical Sunday dinner might feature juicy Rinderrouladen, creamy Kartoffelpuree, and sweet Apfelkuchen.

50. What change should be made to sentence 27?

a. Insert *that* after *Bakeries*
b. Insert *big* after *of*
c. Insert *everything* after *selling*
d. Insert *and* after *to*

51. What change, if any, should be made to sentence 29?

a. Change *Americaner* to *Amerikaner*
b. Change *name* to *names*
c. Change *City's* to *Cities*
d. No change

Written Composition

Write an essay about something you have learned that changed your outlook on life.

Answers and Explanations

1. D: In paragraph 22, Mrs. Bennet insists that Mr. Bennet must go and see Mr. Bingley once he moves into the neighborhood, but Mr. Bennet refuses in paragraph 23. In paragraph 24, Mrs. Bennet explains why she wants Mr. Bennet to go visit Mr. Bingley. Choice A is not correct because even though Mrs. Bennet is hoping her daughters will meet Mr. Bingley, she first wants Mr. Bennet to make a visit. Although Mr. Bennet uses the word 'engage,' choice B is incorrect because the word 'engage' in this sentence is referring to what Mr. Bingley is hoping for, not wedding engagements. Mrs. Bennet mentions Sir William and Lady Lucas in paragraph 24, but choice C is incorrect because, although she mentions them as a way to convince Mr. Bennet to visit Mr. Bingley, the paragraphs are not chiefly about Sir William and Lady Lucas.

2. C: Because the story is chiefly about Mrs. Bennet's efforts to convince her husband to visit Mr. Bingley and her surprise when he does so. Although choice A describes some aspects of the story, it is not true that both Mr. and Mrs. Bennet go to Netherfield Park. Choice B also has some correct elements, but Mr. Bennet does not take Mrs. Bennet and his daughters to Netherfield Park; instead, he simply tells them about his visit. While it's true that the family discusses an upcoming ball, choice D is incorrect because Mrs. Bennet's main goal is for one of her daughters to marry Mr. Bingley, not for them to get invitations to the ball.

3. B: The correct answer choice is B, *a goal, purpose, or intention*. In paragraph 17, Mr. Bennet asks Mrs. Bennet if Mr. Bingley's design, or plan, in moving to Netherfield Park is to marry one of the Bennets' daughters. *Design* does not mean a treacherous plot because Mr. Bingley's designs are not seen as dangerous. In fact, Mrs. Bennet uses *design* when she tells Mr. Bennet that she doesn't think Mr. Bingley plans to marry one of their daughters but that she certainly hopes he will. While *design* often refers to a sketch or organization of a work of art, it is used here to indicate Mr. Bingley's intentions.

4. B: because Mrs. Bennet makes it clear in paragraphs 14 and 16 that she is looking for a husband for her daughters when she says, "You must know that I am thinking of marrying them." While Mrs. Bennet does want to meet Mr. Bingley, choice A is incorrect because her main goal is to get her daughters married, and meeting Mr. Bingley will help her achieve this goal. Choice C is also incorrect because the events at the dance will not help Mrs. Bennet achieve her main goal, although it will bring her closer to it. Choice D is incorrect because Mrs. Bennet wants Mr. Bennet to go alone to Netherfield Park to meet Mr. Bingley.

5. C: because it shows Mr. Bennet making a joke. The dry, sarcastic sentence shows that Mr. Bennet's sense of humor involves mocking them slightly. Choice A is incorrect because Mr. Bennet is not responding to Mrs. Bennet at that moment. This lack of response does not show humor. Choice B is incorrect because Mrs. Bennet is speaking and complaining about the ways in which Mr. Bennet annoys her. Although choice D talks about Mr. Bennet's sarcastic humor, it is incorrect because it does not show it.

6. A: because paragraph 34 says that Mrs. Bennet's solace (which means comfort) is to visit and hear news, or gossip. Although part of choice B, hearing news, is correct, the passage does not indicate that Mrs. Bennet takes comfort (or solace) from planning her daughters' marriages. Choice C is incorrect because Mrs. Bennet shows more interest in managing her daughters' lives rather than spending time with them. Choice D is incorrect because it only discusses one of the things that Mrs. Bennet takes comfort in.

7. C: because Mrs. Bennet is clearly following strict rules of behavior. She most likely does not live in a contemporary time period because she is relying on her husband to introduce her and her daughters to the new neighbor rather than going there herself. Choice A is incorrect because the passage does not indicate which country the story is set in. Furthermore, the strict social rules imply that the story is taking place in the past. Although Mrs. Bennet does seem to be following strict customs, choice B is incorrect because the passage does not indicate that the family lives in a castle or luxurious setting. Choice D is incorrect because the strict social rules show that the Bennets are not a modern or contemporary family.

8. B: is the correct answer because Mrs. Bennet complains in paragraph 55 that she is sick of Mr. Bingley. In paragraph 58, she changes her mind and is ecstatic that Mr. Bennet visited Mr. Bingley. Choice A is incorrect because it only shows Mrs. Bennet's first reaction. Choice C is incorrect because the word *sick* in paragraph 55 refers to Mrs. Bennet's frustration rather than an illness. Choice D is incorrect because it only addresses Mrs. Bennet's initial frustration and not her later excitement.

9. D: because Mrs. Bennet says in paragraph 40 that Mrs. Long is selfish and hypocritical. Even though Mrs. Bennet then says that she has no opinion of Mrs. Long, choice A is incorrect because Mrs. Bennet does not mean that she doesn't have an opinion, but that she does not have a positive opinion. Choice B is incorrect because Mrs. Bennet thinks that Mrs. Long is selfish in addition to being dishonest. Choice C is incorrect because Mrs. Bennet does not indicate that she thinks Mrs. Long has become a generous person.

10. D: because the phrase *universally acknowledged* means something that most people accept as truth or fact. Choice A is incorrect because the word *truth* refers to a fact rather than an opinion. Choice B is incorrect because Mrs. Bennet's goal is to find a husband for her daughters. However, Mrs. Bennet also believes in this truth and thinks that Mr. Bingley is looking for a wife himself. While Mr. and Mrs. Bennet might believe in the truth, choice C is incorrect because the word *universally* means that all or most people believe the truth as well.

11. B: is correct because paragraph 34 consists entirely of a description of Mr. and Mrs. Bennets' personalities. Choice A is incorrect because the paragraph only describes Mrs. Bennet's goals and not her deeper motivations. Choice C is incorrect because the paragraph does not have any dialogue. Choice D is incorrect because the paragraph simply says that she wants her daughters married without explaining why.

12. B: because the word *beneficence* is used to show how nature helps the plants and animals on earth. For example, nature provides that sun and rain that helps the trees grow. Choice A is incorrect because *beneficence* is referring to the way in which nature helps life grow. Choice C is incorrect because nature gives the sun and the rain, making it the opposite of stingy. Although the narrator later experiences the dangers of nature, choice D is incorrect because paragraph 11 is about the generosity of nature.

13. D: because the two paragraphs show the narrator's discovery that words have meaning. Choice A is incorrect because neither the narrator nor Miss Sullivan uses a pencil. Instead, Miss Sullivan uses her fingers to spell words into the narrator's hand. Although the narrator learns about the difference between a mug and water, choice B is incorrect because the main idea of the paragraphs is that the narrator learns that words have meaning. Choice C is incorrect because the temper tantrum is just one small part of the two paragraphs.

14. A: because Helen says in the second sentence that she stretched out her hand "as I supposed to my mother." Choice B is incorrect because Helen does not yet know that a visitor is coming. Choice C is incorrect because Helen says she held out her hand as she would to her mother, not that she wants to please her mother. Choice D is incorrect because Helen does not yet know the visitor.

15. B: because Helen is alone and defenseless as the storm approaches. Choice A is incorrect because Helen is not lost; she knows where she is but is unable to get out of the tree and get home. Although wind and approaching rain may make Helen feel uncomfortable, choices C and D are incorrect because Helen's main nervousness comes from being alone and wanting the presence of her teacher, Miss Sullivan.

16. C: because Miss Sullivan opened up Helen's world by showing her that words have meaning and that every object has a name. Choice A is incorrect because the specific words that Miss Sullivan taught Helen are not as important as the overall concept of words. Choice B is incorrect because the observation about barriers is not what she learned from Miss Sullivan. Choice D is incorrect because the sentence is not about what Helen learned, but about the concept of learning itself.

17. D: because Helen's relief at feeling Miss Sullivan's arms shows her reliance on and love for Miss Sullivan. Choice A is incorrect because Miss Sullivan first spells d-o-l-l at the beginning of their relationship; they have not yet developed a close bond. Choice B is incorrect because Helen cries when she suddenly discovers what her behavior means, not because of Miss Sullivan. Choice C is incorrect because it does not show the bond between Helen and Miss Sullivan; instead, this moment simply shows something Helen and Miss Sullivan are doing together.

18. B: because the passage shows Helen's discovery of language and communication. While Helen develops a close tie with Miss Sullivan, Miss Sullivan is not Helen's family, making choice A incorrect. Choice C is incorrect because the passage is about Helen's joy of learning and close bond with Miss Sullivan rather than any disappointment. Choice D is incorrect because the passage is about bonds and learning rather than youth.

19. D: is correct because the paragraph is about the way in which nature is turning on Helen and becoming cruel. Choice A is incorrect because Miss Sullivan does not show any cruelty towards Helen. Choice B is incorrect because this paragraph shows Helen feeling nervous but does not show her having a temper tantrum. Choice C is incorrect because Helen was in danger from being alone in the tree as the storm approached; the phrase *treacherous claws* refers to the danger of being alone in the tree rather than the danger of climbing the tree itself.

20. A: because the story shows Helen just before meeting Miss Sullivan and then shows the effect that Miss Sullivan has on Helen's life. Although Helen may have learned to control some of her temper tantrums, the order of events in the story is intended to show Helen's growing relationship with Miss Sullivan, making choice B incorrect. Choice C is incorrect because only part of the passage shows the strategies Miss Sullivan used to teach Helen. Choice D is incorrect because Helen feels security rather than confusion when she's with Miss Sullivan.

21. C: is correct because the passage is about how Miss Sullivan taught Helen that words have meaning. Choice A is incorrect because Helen indicates that she loves Miss Sullivan. Choice B is incorrect because Helen is not scared of nature; rather, she realizes that nature can be both generous and dangerous. Although the passage does not explicitly say that Helen learns to read or write, it shows the beginning of her relationship with words and implies that Helen will continue to learn.

22. A: because it explains how Helen was locked in a world where she couldn't communicate or express herself before Miss Sullivan arrived. Choice B is incorrect because it does not illustrate Helen's state of being; instead, the sentence simply says that Helen didn't know what the future held. Choice C is incorrect because the sentence shows that Helen knew something unusual was happening but does not show the way in which Helen was constrained. Choice D is incorrect because it simply illustrates one of Helen's first encounters with her teacher.

23. C: Even though Mrs. Bennet and Helen are very different characters with different motivations and challenges, they both display frustration in their selections. Mrs. Bennet is frustrated when Mr. Bennet refuses to see Mr. Bingley, and Helen is frustrated when Miss Sullivan won't do what she wants. Choice A is incorrect because both Helen and Mrs. Bennet hope to be understood by their companions. Choice B is incorrect because both Helen and Mrs. Bennet eventually get what they want. Choice D is incorrect because, while they may both encounter big changes, they don't show that they are looking forward to these changes.

24. B: is correct because both passages have a theme of hope. Mrs. Bennet deeply hopes that her daughters will find husbands, and Helen hopes to continue learning how to communicate with words. Although Helen learns, choice A is incorrect because the excerpt of "Pride and Prejudice" does not contain examples of learning. Choice C is incorrect because neither passage focuses on the struggle between good and evil. Choice D is incorrect because both passages end on notes of hope rather than despair.

25. D: is correct because both Mr. and Mrs. Bennet and Helen and Miss Sullivan show care and affection. Mr. and Mrs. Bennet constantly bicker, but in the end, Mr. Bennet shows that he cares about his wife by visiting Mr. Bingley. Helen and Miss Sullivan undertake a voyage of discovery through learning and also exhibit deep care for each other. Choices A and B are incorrect because choice A is only true of Mr. and Mrs. Bennet and choice B is only true of Helen and Miss Sullivan. Choice C is incorrect because it is not true of either relationship.

26. D: because *receipt* in this context means *to receive*. The advertiser is saying that it must receive three postage stamps before it will send the material samples and self-measurement directions. Choice A is the most common definition of *receipt*, but it is incorrect because the reader has not bought anything yet. Choice B is incorrect because *receipt* is referring to the advertiser receiving three stamps, not a piece of paper. Choice C is incorrect because the name of cooking instructions is *recipe*, not *receipt*.

27. B: is the correct answer. The advertiser is promoting custom-made dresses delivered through the mail. In order for customers to get the right size, they need to measure themselves accurately. Choice A is incorrect because the advertisement only mentioned the "latest style." However, it does not indicate that customers can choose their own styles. Choice C is incorrect because the customer does not measure the cloth her or himself. Choice D is incorrect because the advertisement makes it clear that the advertiser will make the dresses, not the customer.

28. A: is correct because the advertiser is giving the reader incentives to purchase additional items in order to complete a trousseau or wardrobe. Choice B is incorrect because clothes for infants and children are mentioned above rather than near this sentence. Choice C is incorrect because the previous sentence is the sentence that says that all inquiries are answered. Choice D is incorrect because the sentence lists the types clothing collections customers can purchase, but not the types of materials that are available to be used.

29. Sample Answer:

Mr. and Mrs. Bennet are a married couple who argue a lot. They don't fully understand each other's motivations, which leads to them arguing back and forth. For example, in paragraph 16, Mrs. Bennet asks Mr. Bennet how he can be so tiresome. She's irritated that he doesn't understand her excitement about Mr. Bingley's arrival. Even though Mr. and Mrs. Bennet bicker for most of the passage, they have a deep and loving relationship. Mr. Bennet initially refuses to visit Mr. Bingley, even though Mrs. Bennet practically begs him to do so. However, Mr. Bennet eventually visits Mr. Bingley because he knows that it's important to his wife. He takes delight in teasing her, such as when he says "But I hope you will get over it, and live to see many young men of four thousand a year come into the neighborhood." Underneath his teasing, he cares for his wife and wants to please her, which is why he goes to see Mr. Bingley.

30. Sample Answer:

Helen says that before Miss Sullivan arrives, her life was like being "at sea in a dense fog" (paragraph 3). She was unable to communicate effectively with others and had a minimal connection with the outside world. Miss Sullivan helped open up Helen's world by teaching her the power of words. It took Helen some time to realize that words and meaning were connected. However, once Helen realized this, her world opened up. She says in paragraph 7, "That living word awakened my soul, gave it light, hope, joy, set it free!" This sentence means that understanding words helped her to improve her communication with the world and to express herself. Miss Sullivan is directly responsible for helping Helen learn the meaning of words, which is why Helen says that the day Miss Sullivan arrived was the most important day of her life.

31. Sample Answer:

Even though Mr. and Mrs. Bennet are married, I think that Helen and Miss Sullivan have a closer relationship because Miss Sullivan's teaching completely transformed Helen's life and her understanding of the world. In paragraph 1 of "The Story of My Life," Helen says the day Miss Sullivan arrived was the most important of her life. She then goes on to explain the way in which Miss Sullivan taught Helen the meaning of words. The scene that best depicts Helen and Miss Sullivan's close relationship is in paragraph 14, when Helen is alone and scared in the tree. When she feels Miss Sullivan's arms around her, Helen feels safe and secure. Mr. and Mrs. Bennet may also have a close relationship, but it is marred by their constant bickering, such as when they're arguing over whether or not Mr. Bennet should visit Mr. Bingley. This bickering shows that Mr. and Mrs. Bennet don't depend on each other as much as Helen depends on Miss Sullivan.

32. C: because a comma should not be used to separate the sentence's subject (Paul Revere) and verb (ran). Choice A is incorrect because an apostrophe would make *1760s* possessive, which it is not. Choice B is incorrect because the comma is used to separate a nonessential clause from the rest of the sentence. Choice D is incorrect because the words *busy* and *metalworking* are not merely a series of adjectives. Instead, *busy* is an adjective modifying the noun *metalworking shop.*

33. C: because *British* is a proper noun and should always be capitalized. Choice A is incorrect because the passage is written in past tense; therefore, *got* should remain in past tense. Choice B is incorrect because the sentence is referring to something getting worse, rather than something that is the superlative *worst.* Choice D is incorrect because *Stamp Act* is a proper noun.

34. C: is the correct answer because *stamp* in this sentence is not a proper noun and does not need to be capitalized. In this context, *stamp* only needs to be capitalized when it is used in the name *Stamp Act*. Choice A is incorrect because the comma sets off a non-essential phrase at the beginning of the sentence. Choice B is incorrect because the comma sets off the initial dependent clause from the independent clause in the second half of the sentence. Choice D is incorrect because *signed contract* is not a proper noun or formal name.

35. A: because *were* is referring to the plural noun colonists. As a singular verb form, *was* is incorrect in this case. Choice B is incorrect because *parliament* is the correct spelling. Choice C is incorrect because the comma is required to set off the nonessential phrase that follows. Choice D is incorrect because *that* is used to set off a restrictive clause and should not be preceded by a comma.

36. B: because a comma and conjunction are correctly used to separate two independent clauses. Although choice A has the conjunction *and*, it is missing the required comma. Choice C is incorrect because no comma is required when a single subject (*colonists*) is shared by two predicates. Choice D is incorrect because the comma creates a run-on sentence.

37. C: because a comma should not be used to separate independent clauses from essential phrases that begin with *that*. Choice A is incorrect because the Sons of Liberty staged multiple demonstrations. The reader can determine this because there is no article before the word *demonstrations*. Choice B is incorrect because a comma is not needed to separate an independent clause from a dependent clause when the clauses are connected by a conjunction. Choice D is incorrect because the tree was *in* the city of Boston, not *at* a specific location.

38. B: because a comma is needed to separate the dependent clause beginning with the word *after* from the independent clause beginning with *Paul*. Choice A is incorrect because the comma would divide a clause. Choice C is incorrect because *received* is the correct spelling. Choice D is incorrect because a comma is required after the word *Act*.

39. C: because the phrase *lighting up the sky* is non-essential and should be separated from the rest of the sentence by a comma. While the number *280* could be written out, choice A is incorrect because it should be written as *two hundred and eighty*. Choice C is incorrect because *tree's* is possessive and requires the apostrophe. Choice D is incorrect because *nightly* is an adverb, which should modify a verb. However, the word is modifying a noun and must be written as an adjective.

40. A: because a comma should be used to separate the independent clause beginning with *some members* from the non-essential phrase beginning with *which is*. Choice B is incorrect because it is missing the comma. Choice C incorrectly uses *that* instead of *which*. Choice D is incorrect because it uses a semicolon instead of a comma.

41. B: because a semicolon should be used to separate two independent clauses. Choice A is incorrect because *may* provides important meaning to the sentence. Choice C is incorrect because the comma correctly separates the two clauses. Choice D is incorrect because the passage is talking about a figure from history and should use the past tense.

42. C: because the word *together* reinforces the word *join* but is not required; *joined together* is slightly redundant. Choice A is incorrect because the year is required to help the reader know when these events are taking place. Choice B is incorrect because the phrase *from both sides of the city* tells the reader that citizens from both East Berlin and West Berlin participated. Choice D is incorrect because *break down* makes it clear that the wall was torn down.

43. C: because *Berlin* is a possessive that modifies *buildings* (the buildings are in Berlin). Choice A is incorrect because the word *however* is a conjunctive that should stand on its own and be followed by a comma. The word *although* correctly sets up the dependent clause that begins the sentence. Choice B is incorrect because *during World War II* is part of the subject and should not be separated by a comma from the verb *destroyed*. Choice D is incorrect because the verb should be the present tense *has*. Present tense is required because the city is still rebuilt.

44. D: because the article *a* indicates that *symbol* should be singular rather than plural. Choice A is incorrect because *gate* is part of the proper noun *Brandenburg Gate*. Choice B is incorrect because the subject of the sentence is singular, which means the verb must be singular. Choice C is incorrect because a comma is not required after the year because it is essential to the sentence.

45. B: because the conjunction *and* is separating two independent clauses. When this happens, a comma is required before the conjunction. Choice A is incorrect because the sentence is talking about *years*, which is plural, rather than possessive. Choice C is incorrect because a comma is not needed between the *and* in a two-item series. Choice D is incorrect because the subject *tensions* is plural, which means the verb *were* needs to remain in the plural form.

46. C: because the conjunction *and* connects an independent clause and a dependent clause. When these two types of clauses are connected, a comma should not be used. Choice A is not correct because the prepositional phrase *in the audience* is essential and should not be separated by commas. Choices B and D are incorrect because both words are spelled correctly in the original passage.

47. D: because a comma should not separate an adjective from the noun it modifies. Choice A is incorrect because the word *German* is an adjective that is correctly modifying *cuisine*, while *Germany* is a noun. Choice B is incorrect because the sentence is constructed as a passive sentence and needs the passive verb form *is known*. Choice C is incorrect because *it's* means *it is* and is not a possessive.

48. D: because a comma and the conjunction *and* are required to combine the sentences. *And* is a better choice than *but* because the second sentence is a continuation of the first rather than a contradiction. Choices A and B are incorrect because the conjunction *but* doesn't fit the meaning of the sentences. Choice A is also missing the required comma. Choice C uses the correct conjunction, *and*, but is missing the comma.

49. B: is correct because it uses parentheses to define the German words. This version is both the least wordy choice and also one that defines the unknown words. Choices A and C also define the unknown words, but they are longer and wordier than choice B. Choice C is the most concise, but it does not define the German words, which might confuse a reader who does not understand German.

50. C: because the word *everything* is the object of the clause and the sentence would be incomplete without it. Choice A is incorrect because the word *that* would turn the first part of the sentence into a complex subject rather than a subject and verb. Choice B is incorrect because *big* changes the meaning of the sentence. While the towns may be big, it is not required to fix the sentence. Choice D is incorrect because *rich* is an adjective that modifies the noun *pastries*; these words should not be separated by *and*.

51. A: is the correct answer because *Amerikaner* should be spelled with a 'k.' The reader can determine this spelling by looking at the previous sentence. Choice B is incorrect because *name* is referring to a singular subject. Choice C is incorrect because the word *City's* should be singular possessive, not plural. Choice D is incorrect because it misspells *Amerikaner* as *Americaner*.

Sample Written Composition

When I was in fourth grade, my best friend, Kayla, moved away. Kayla and I had been friends since we first met in preschool. We were inseparable – two peas in a pod – and I was devastated when I learned that her mom was being transferred to a job hundreds of miles away. Kayla and I had dozens of sleepovers in the months before she moved. We plotted ways to stay in touch after she left, such as email, instant message, text, and even old-fashioned letters. We made special email accounts that would only be used for each other's emails, and we devised secret code words that we would use when we needed to say something important or private.

When Kayla left at the beginning of summer break, I cried for hours. She sent me constant texts from the car, telling me about what she was seeing and how sad she was to be moving. When she arrived in her new town, she took pictures of all the rooms in her new house, the mall, the supermarket, and even the gas station. For a few months, we stayed in constant touch.

Then school started, and things changed. I was suddenly busy with gymnastics and ballet three days a week. Kayla took gymnastics and ballet, too, but she lived two time zones away. When I was finishing my after-school activities for the day, she was starting hers. We started talking, texting, and emailing less and less.

One day I realized that I'd gone two weeks without talking to Kayla. That's when I learned something that changed my outlook on life. Being friends isn't always easy. Kayla and I had been close friends for years and I wanted to stay best friends with her for the rest of my life. But if I wanted to keep her as a best friend, I needed to make a constant effort to stay in touch, to stay connected. That day, I sent Kayla a quick text after gymnastics, telling her about a new move I'd learned. She replied a few hours later with a picture from her gymnastics class. From then on, I made sure to send Kayla a message every day, even when I was tired or didn't have anything to say. Five years later, we're still best friends. I'm even going to visit her this summer.

I realized that if you want something, you need to work hard for it. I've applied this lesson to many areas of my life. For example, my goal is to go to a top college. I know that means I need to get very good grades and that I need to study even when I'm tired and not in the mood. I force myself to study, and that's helping me meet my goal. In fact, I'm hoping that Kayla and I go to the same college. But even if we don't, I know we'll stay in touch and still be best friends.

Practice Test #2

Practice Questions

Alice's Adventures in Wonderland

By Lewis Carroll

QUESTIONS 1 -11 PERTAIN TO THE FOLLOWING PASSAGES:

Alice was beginning to get very tired of sitting by her sister on the bank, and of having nothing to do: once or twice she had peeped into the book her sister was reading, but it had no pictures or conversations in it, 'and what is the use of a book,' thought Alice 'without pictures or conversation?'

So she was considering in her own mind (as well as she could, for the hot day made her feel very sleepy and stupid), whether the pleasure of making a daisy-chain would be worth the trouble of getting up and picking the daisies, when suddenly a White Rabbit with pink eyes ran close by her.

There was nothing so VERY remarkable in that; nor did Alice think it so VERY much out of the way to hear the Rabbit say to itself, 'Oh dear! Oh dear! I shall be late!' (when she thought it over afterwards, it occurred to her that she ought to have wondered at this, but at the time it all seemed quite natural); but when the Rabbit actually TOOK A WATCH OUT OF ITS WAISTCOAT-POCKET, and looked at it, and then hurried on, Alice started to her feet, for it flashed across her mind that she had never before seen a rabbit with either a waistcoat-pocket, or a watch to take out of it, and burning with curiosity, she ran across the field after it, and fortunately was just in time to see it pop down a large rabbit-hole under the hedge.

In another moment down went Alice after it, never once considering how in the world she was to get out again.

The rabbit-hole went straight on like a tunnel for some way, and then dipped suddenly down, so suddenly that Alice had not a moment to think about stopping herself before she found herself falling down a very deep well.

Either the well was very deep, or she fell very slowly, for she had plenty of time as she went down to look about her and to wonder what was going to happen next. First, she tried to look down and make out what she was coming to, but it was too dark to see anything; then she looked at the sides of the well, and noticed that they were filled with cupboards and book-shelves; here and there she saw maps and pictures hung upon pegs. She took down a jar from one of the shelves as she passed; it was labelled 'ORANGE MARMALADE', but to her great disappointment it was empty: she did not like to drop the jar for fear of killing somebody, so managed to put it into one of the cupboards as she fell past it.

'Well!' thought Alice to herself, 'after such a fall as this, I shall think nothing of tumbling down stairs! How brave they'll all think me at home! Why, I wouldn't say anything about it, even if I fell off the top of the house!' (Which was very likely true.)

Down, down, down. Would the fall NEVER come to an end! 'I wonder how many miles I've fallen by this time?' she said aloud. 'I must be getting somewhere near the centre of the earth. Let me see: that would be four thousand miles down, I think—' (for, you see, Alice had learnt several things of this sort in her lessons in the schoolroom, and though this was not a VERY good opportunity for showing off her knowledge, as there was no one to listen to her, still it was good practice to say it over) '—yes, that's about the right distance—but then I wonder what Latitude or Longitude I've got to?' (Alice had no idea what Latitude was, or Longitude either, but thought they were nice grand words to say.)

Presently she began again. 'I wonder if I shall fall right THROUGH the earth! How funny it'll seem to come out among the people that walk with their heads downward! The Antipathies, I think—' (she was rather glad there WAS no one listening, this time, as it didn't sound at all the right word) '—but I shall have to ask them what the name of the country is, you know. Please, Ma'am, is this New Zealand or Australia?' (and she tried to curtsey as she spoke—fancy CURTSEYING as you're falling through the air! Do you think you could manage it?) 'And what an ignorant little girl she'll think me for asking! No, it'll never do to ask: perhaps I shall see it written up somewhere.'

Down, down, down. There was nothing else to do, so Alice soon began talking again. 'Dinah'll miss me very much to-night, I should think!' (Dinah was the cat.) 'I hope they'll remember her saucer of milk at tea-time. Dinah my dear! I wish you were down here with me! There are no mice in the air, I'm afraid, but you might catch a bat, and that's very like a mouse, you know. But do cats eat bats, I wonder?' And here Alice began to get rather sleepy, and went on saying to herself, in a dreamy sort of way, 'Do cats eat bats? Do cats eat bats?' and sometimes, 'Do bats eat cats?' for, you see, as she couldn't answer either question, it didn't much matter which way she put it. She felt that she was dozing off, and had just begun to dream that she was walking hand in hand with Dinah, and saying to her very earnestly, 'Now, Dinah, tell me the truth: did you ever eat a bat?' when suddenly, thump! thump! down she came upon a heap of sticks and dry leaves, and the fall was over.

Alice was not a bit hurt, and she jumped up on to her feet in a moment: she looked up, but it was all dark overhead; before her was another long passage, and the White Rabbit was still in sight, hurrying down it. There was not a moment to be lost: away went Alice like the wind, and was just in time to hear it say, as it turned a corner, 'Oh my ears and whiskers, how late it's getting!' She was close behind it when she turned the corner, but the Rabbit was no longer to be seen: she found herself in a long, low hall, which was lit up by a row of lamps hanging from the roof.

There were doors all round the hall, but they were all locked; and when Alice had been all the way down one side and up the other, trying every door, she walked sadly down the middle, wondering how she was ever to get out again.

Suddenly she came upon a little three-legged table, all made of solid glass; there was nothing on it except a tiny golden key, and Alice's first thought was that it might belong to one of the doors of the hall; but, alas! either the locks were too large, or the key was too small, but at any rate it would not open any of them. However, on the second time round, she came upon a low curtain she had not noticed before, and behind it was a little door about fifteen inches high: she tried the little golden key in the lock, and to her great delight it fitted!

Alice opened the door and found that it led into a small passage, not much larger than a rat-hole: she knelt down and looked along the passage into the loveliest garden you ever saw. How she longed to get out of that dark hall, and wander about among those beds of bright flowers and those cool fountains, but she could not even get her head through the doorway; 'and even if my head would go through,' thought poor Alice, 'it would be of very little use without my shoulders. Oh, how I wish I could shut up like a telescope! I think I could, if I only know how to begin.' For, you see, so many out-of-the-way things had happened lately, that Alice had begun to think that very few things indeed were really impossible.

There seemed to be no use in waiting by the little door, so she went back to the table, half hoping she might find another key on it, or at any rate a book of rules for shutting people up like telescopes: this time she found a little bottle on it, ('which certainly was not here before,' said Alice,) and round the neck of the bottle was a paper label, with the words 'DRINK ME' beautifully printed on it in large letters.

It was all very well to say 'Drink me,' but the wise little Alice was not going to do THAT in a hurry. 'No, I'll look first,' she said, 'and see whether it's marked "poison" or not'; for she had read several nice little histories about children who had got burnt, and eaten up by wild beasts and other unpleasant things, all because they WOULD not remember the simple rules their friends had taught them: such as, that a red-hot poker will burn you if you hold it too long; and that if you cut your finger VERY deeply with a knife, it usually bleeds; and she had never forgotten that, if you drink much from a bottle marked 'poison,' it is almost certain to disagree with you, sooner or later.

However, this bottle was NOT marked 'poison,' so Alice ventured to taste it, and finding it very nice, (it had, in fact, a sort of mixed flavour of cherry-tart, custard, pine-apple, roast turkey, toffee, and hot buttered toast,) she very soon finished it off.

'What a curious feeling!' said Alice; 'I must be shutting up like a telescope.'

And so it was indeed: she was now only ten inches high, and her face brightened up at the thought that she was now the right size for going through the little door into that lovely garden. First, however, she waited for a few minutes to see if she was going to shrink any further: she felt a little nervous about this; 'for it might end, you know,' said Alice to herself, 'in my going out altogether, like a candle. I wonder what I should be like then?' And she tried to fancy what the flame of a candle is like after the candle is blown out, for she could not remember ever having seen such a thing.

1. Read the following dictionary entry:

> *Burning* [bur-ning] adjective (1) intense or urgent (2) very hot (3) on fire, with visible flames (4) a feeling caused by some kind of fire or heat

Which definition best matches the meaning of *burning* as it is used in paragraph 3?

a. Definition 1
b. Definition 2
c. Definition 3
d. Definition 4

2. How does the setting at the beginning of the story contribute to Alice's decision to follow the White Rabbit?

a. It makes her feel sleepy
b. It makes her feel restless
c. It makes her feel curious
d. It makes her feel like reading

3. Why might Alice use the words *latitude* and *longitude* in paragraph 8?

a. She wants to find her exact location on the map.
b. She wants to show off her knowledge of big words.
c. She wants to see if her words echo down the hole.
d. She wants to say big words even if she doesn't know exactly what they mean.

4. Why has the author capitalized the words *through*, *was*, and *curtseying* in paragraph 9?

a. To mark them as words that need to be proofread
b. To emphasize their meaning
c. To show that Alice is upset by falling
d. To indicate that Alice is talking to someone

5. Alice's decision to drink the liquid in the bottle in paragraphs 15-17 can be described as...

a. Thoughtful
b. Angry
c. Wild
d. Unreasonable

6. Why does Alice feel nervous in paragraph 19?

a. She thinks the liquid might be poison
b. She is afraid that the liquid isn't working
c. She is worried that she will keep shrinking
d. She is nervous that she will turn into a flame

7. From the description in paragraphs 6-10, the reader can tell that...

a. Alice is in great danger
b. Alice is very nervous
c. The story will be realistic
d. The story will be fantastical

8. What is Alice's problem in paragraph 14?

a. She can't fit the key into any of the doors
b. She can't fit through the door that the key opens
c. She is shrinking
d. She is in a strange, unknown setting

9. What is the author indicating is most unusual about the rabbit described in paragraphs 2 and 3?

a. It has pink eyes
b. It is speaking
c. It has a watch
d. It jumps down a rabbit hole

10. In paragraph 7, why does Alice say "I shall think nothing of tumbling down the stairs!"?

a. She has discovered a way to fall safely
b. She thinks that any future fall will be shorter than the fall through the rabbit hole
c. She is concerned that her clumsiness will lead to many future falls
d. She wants her family to think that she's very brave

11. What does paragraph 4 say about Alice's personality?

a. She's impulsive
b. She's thoughtful
c. She's curious
d. She's sneaky

QUESTIONS 12 – 22 PERTAIN TO THE FOLLOWING LETTER:

Letters from an Oklahoman Abroad

By Carrie LeFlore Perry

Montreal

Mother Mine:

(1) Out of the United States! We passed across the lake from Lewiston to Toronto and finding a couple of hours at our disposal, we proceeded to "do" the town. I cannot say it is especially interesting; it is clean and hustling, but too much like an American city to please me. You see, I am looking for the old, the beautiful and the picturesque, not the new and practical. The night was so cool I slept like a child and awoke at five-thirty ready to enjoy the Thousand Islands. I think a picture of an openmouthed rustic and a whole row of exclamation points would give you a better idea of my state this morning than words. Island after island, bearing homes of splendor, then dear little wooded spots with an unpretentious cottage peeping from the trees; again, a monster club house and magnificent grounds, just one continuous picture of homes and places of pleasure. Many of the houses crowning the islands were such monster affairs the lawns were lost in the river! Do they have babies in those homes? If so, how do they keep them out of the water? Ed chuckled with pleasure over the mental picture of you, on a little pocket-handkerchief lawn, with those irrepressible boys, in a wild endeavor to keep them out of the St. Lawrence!

(2) The early morning light added to the magic beauty of the scene, yet I shall be disappointed if the Rhine is not more entrancing.

(3) The castles are too new, the homes do not show the caress of time; it is like our entire country, great and beautiful, but so new, so palpably new. We were from six to ten-thirty passing through this wonderful bit of the St. Lawrence, and like unto children, we were quite sure the island of the moment was the most fair.

(4) We were told that there were 1,642 in all, and I do not doubt the statement after this morning. Leaving Prescott where we changed to a smaller boat, we were soon passing the numerous rapids. They increased in wonder until the Lachine Rapids were entered, and there we were truly amazed! A lady friend had informed me that I would be greatly disappointed with the rapids, as they were very peaceful, like unto soap bubbles! My comment is this: I would not wish that brand of soap turned loose in my vicinity if I were boating. Do you recall the legend of the Indian, who, for telling a lie, was doomed by the Great Spirit to ever wander by streams with his canoe upon his back in a fruitless search for a place to launch it? I wonder if he ever tried the Lachine Rapids? If he did I'll venture the Great Spirit had to hurry to save man and canoe. When we reached Cornwall, we found the bridge had fallen, blocking the canal, and learned our boat would be the last to Montreal for several days. You see the vessels go down the river but up the canal, because of the rapids. I am so thankful we did not miss our river trip.

(5) We are staying at a quaint old hotel, in the French part of the city, very near the cathedral where Ed was christened. You need a guide in the hotel; it is a succession of up you go and down you come! There is an air of age and an odor too, about the rooms and corridors. We were told the present King stayed here, when he visited Canada as

Prince of Wales, and I feel sure there has been little change since then! We have a monster apartment lined with mirrors and such massive furniture I feel oppressed. I tried to find the office before commencing this letter, and landed in an unknown hall. Seeing a chambermaid I inquired the way to the elevator, and was told something like this: Up two stairs, around a corner, down three steps, a long corridor, up three, then up two, across a hall, and enter the elevator and I would soon find myself opposite the office! I appreciated her directions but begged her to escort me to room 45 as I would defer the excursion until my husband returned.

(6) I wish I could find my way to the hall of the lion; it is rather exciting to press a button, see the monster tongue loll out, and then a stream of ice water. Would not the boys drink to repletion?

June 24

(7) Mother, Ed came in just as I was finishing the above paragraph, and with his assistance I found the lion and also enjoyed a street car ride. Today we have been "sight-seeing." Right here I wish to say that Ed would be a capital guide, he will even sacrifice truth to interest if he is not sure of his data. You would never suspect it, but I have a lurking suspicion that I have been told many dream tales, although what of it? May not a man romance of his home city? The very first thing we did was to make our way across the historic Place D'Armes Square into the old cathedral. It is a place of shadows, where prayer comes easily to the heart; beneath the giant crucifix of our Lord thereon, the soul is melted with tenderness.

(8) I did so wish to examine the records and see his name there, as a tiny infant, but we were too early, and later in the day we would be elsewhere. We had decided to have breakfast in the Café A--, where Ed assured me the delicacies offered were beyond compare, and the room a little palace. Ah, the eyes of childhood! When we entered the small place, Ed with a twinkle said: "My dear, this place has grown smaller; I assure you it used to be the size of the cathedral!" Dear old café, perhaps it had seen better days; I know I have never seen a poorer breakfast. I drank to the King, in a cup of awful liquid called English Breakfast tea. Heaven pity the subjects of King Edward if they drink that decoction frequently! After a most unsatisfactory repast Ed said: "Now we will buy the very finest peppermints in the world; the kind I used to eat." Alas for the dreams of childhood, the candy was the "last straw." When we reached the street it was my turn and I said, "Let us buy presidents at a baker shop, you know dear, the kind you used to buy in old Montreal." You see I was determined to finish the "dream" right then and there. Cruel of me, I hear you say? Do believe me, that pastry was delicious, the very best ever; I shall urge all my friends to visit Montreal and eat "Presidents." We walked on old Bleury Street to the Jesuit College where his young ideas were encourage to burst into bloom, and there I met an old priest who knew Ed as a boy, and had the pleasure (?) of teaching him. He assured me that Ed's ideas were always ready to bloom and ofttimes the flowers were startling.

(9) No one feared he would die early because of his angelic goodness, but they often expected him to enter the pearly gates in a violent manner. He was permitted to lead me through his former class room, recreation room, and out-door play grounds; it was quite interesting to see the places and hear his animated tales of old school days.

(10) From the College to Mount Royal on the cars it is but a little time, and there we were high above the city, enjoying the wondrous panorama. Ed pointed out all the historic houses and thus I have learned my Montreal fairly well, even if here but a day. This is a city of churches and charitable institutions, if we had more time we would surely visit many of them; I am not fully content with a "bird's eye view." When we returned to the hotel, while I rested Ed went out to see a college chum who is now a dignified attorney; he must have had a jolly time as he was quite late returning to the hotel for me, and our little excursion to the Convent of the Ladies of the Sacred Heart was begun as the afternoon was almost ended.

(11) The trolley ride was so cool and through such fine country I was rather sorry when the convent cross appeared. Madame K., my old teacher, gave us welcome and showed us the many beauties of the place. It was such a comfort to talk with dear Madam, I felt that she was truly interested in all that concerned me. After a pleasant hour, we turned our faces towards Montreal; the lamps were glowing when we reached the city and thus our pleasure was enhanced, it lies so quaint and queer under the gleaming lights. After a dinner--not at the Café A.--we strolled along the streets of the French town and Ed aired his mother-tongue with the many children scampering here and there in the joys of hide and seek. Thus ends our day in Montreal; we are true birds of passage, in twenty minutes we leave for Quebec, and until then you will have peace.

Lovingly,

C.

12. In paragraph 8, the word *repast* refers to...

a. English Breakfast tea
b. Breakfast
c. Peppermints
d. King Edward

13. Paragraphs 1-3 are mainly about the narrator...

a. Sightseeing across the United States
b. Exploring the castles along the Rhine river
c. Going down the St. Lawrence river to see both mansions and cottages
d. Watching children play in the river

14. Why does the narrator find the Thousand Islands to be disappointing?

a. She thinks that the homes don't look old enough
b. She is displeased that the cottages and castles are so old
c. She is angry that the name of the islands is the Thousand Islands when there are really 1,642 islands
d. There were too many children around

15. How did the narrator learn about Montreal?

a. By touring the Thousand Islands
b. By eating at Café A
c. By viewing the city from Mount Royal
d. By chatting with Madame K.

16. Which sentence best explains why Ed thought the breakfast at Café A would be delicious?

a. I know I have never seen a poorer breakfast
b. Heaven pity the subjects of King Edward if they drink that decoction frequently
c. Do believe me, that pastry was delicious, the very best ever
d. Ah, the eyes of childhood!

17. What is the narrator's purpose in writing this selection?

a. To write a travel book
b. To visit Montreal
c. To remember her childhood
d. To describe her visit to Montreal

18. In paragraph 8, why does the narrator place a question mark after the word *pleasure*?

a. She is unsure if she spelled the word correctly
b. She has not decided if she likes the priest
c. She jokingly thinks that it would have been unpleasant to teach Ed
d. She is not sure if the priest was really Ed's teacher

19. The narrator's description of Montreal shows that she is...

a. An enthusiastic tourist
b. Irritated at having to travel
c. Homesick for her mother
d. Impatient to move on to Quebec

20. After reading paragraphs 8, 9, and 10, the reader can determine that...

a. It was Ed and the narrator's first time in Montreal.
b. Ed grew up in Montreal.
c. The narrator dislikes Montreal.
d. The narrator knows everything there is to know about Montreal.

21. In paragraph 4, why does the narrator recall a legend?

a. She is feeling homesick and wants to remember the stories of her youth.
b. She is comparing the main character from the legend to the Lachine Rapids.
c. She is joking that if the main character from the legend had to take the Lachine Rapids, the Great Spirit would have needed to rescue him.
d. She compares the legend to the fallen bridge.

22. In paragraph 8, what does the word *Presidents* refer to?

a. Pastries
b. The President of the United States
c. A dream
d. The bakery

USE "ALICE'S ADVENTURES IN WONDERLAND" AND "LETTERS FROM AN OKLAHOMAN" TO ANSWER QUESTIONS 23-25:

23. What is something that Alice from *Alice's Adventures in Wonderland* and the narrator of *Letters from an Oklahoman Abroad* have in common?

a. They are both traveling with companions
b. They are both experiencing something new
c. They are both seeing strange, fantastical things
d. They are both journeying by boat

24. What emotion does the narrator of Letters from an Oklahoman Abroad and Alice from Alice's Adventures in Wonderland share?

a. Curiosity
b. Fear
c. Disappointment
d. Excitement

25. The two passages both contain...

a. Unique animals.
b. Memories.
c. Historic buildings.
d. A journey.

QUESTIONS 26-28 PERTAIN TO THE FOLLOWING VISUAL REPRESENTATION:

Aisha is packing for a trip. See her list below:

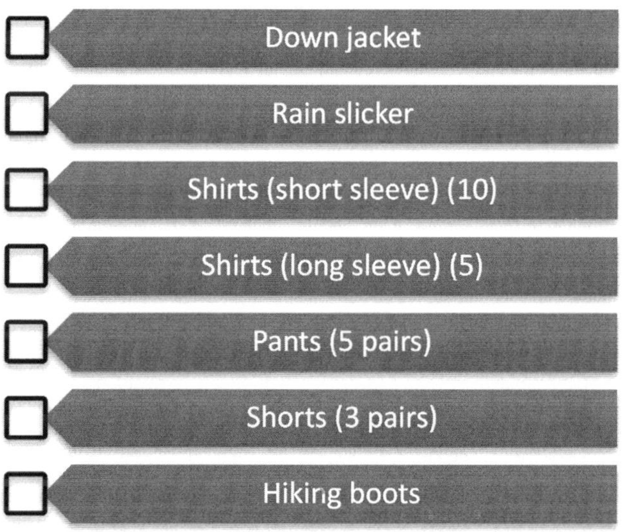

26. Based on the list of items, where could the reader infer Aisha might be going?

a. The rainforest
b. The desert
c. The mountains
d. A tropical beach

27. What's the most logical reason why Aisha might be packing more short sleeve shirts than long sleeve ones?

a. She's worried that some of the short sleeve shirts will get lost
b. She thinks it's more likely to be hot than cold
c. She only has five long sleeve shirts
d. She doesn't want to run out of room in her suitcase

28. If Aisha wanted to pack one more item, which answer below is the most logical choice?

a. A hat
b. A skirt
c. Sandals
d. A wool coat

SHORT ANSWER QUESTIONS

29. In "Alice's Adventures in Wonderland," what techniques does the author use to illustrate Alice's personality? Use examples from the text to explain your answer.

30. In "Letters from an Oklahoman Abroad," do you think that the narrator is eager to continue traveling, or homesick for Oklahoma? Explain your answer using examples from the text.

31. Who has a more adventurous spirit, Alice in "Alice's Adventures in Wonderland" or the narrator in "Letters from an Oklahoman Abroad"? Explain your answer and support it with examples from both selections.

REVISING AND EDITING TEXT 1

QUESTIONS 32 – 41 PERTAIN TO THE FOLLOWING INTRODUCTION AND PASSAGE:

Margot's high school may be adopting a dress code. Margot is against this idea and has written an article for her school newspaper arguing against the dress code. Margot wrote the article and would like your help revising and improving the essay. After you read the article, answer the questions that follow.

(1) Mrs. Conwer, the Jackson High principal, announced last week that Jackson High is considering a student dress code. (2) She is saying that some of the students are wearing outfits to school is being distracting and inappropriate. (3) For example, she says that some of the boys like to wear their pants too low and that some of the girls like to wear very short skirts. (4) I don't agree that there is a problem. (5) Furthermore, I think there are several reasons why it is important that Jackson High does not have a dress code.

(6) When people are in high school, they are teenagers. (7) Being a teenager means that your at a time in life when you are exploring new things and learning about yourself. (8) Many teens also like to express themselves. (9) For example, some people I know keep a blog where they write about things that are important to them. (10) Other people play in a band and can express themselves through music. (11) A lot of teens express themselves through fashion. (12) Since many teens start earning their own money, they can buy their own clothes and choose the fashions that they want. (13) If Jackson High adopts a dress code the students won't be able to express themselves. (14) Self expression are important and is often taught at Jackson High. (15) Ms. Riley, my dance teacher, tells me to express myself through dance. (16) Mr. Hunter, my English teacher, tells me to express myself through writing. (17) Taking

away expression through fashion is hypocritical because it goes against what is taught in many classes.

(18) A dress code at Jackson High will never please everyone. (19) Who gets to decide what is appropriate and what is not? (20) What happens if the students disagree with the code? (21) In school, we learn about respecting different opinions and making compromises. (22) However, if Mrs. Conwer or just a couple of teacher's choose the dress code, they will be ignoring the students. (23) Jackson High should stop ignoring the lessons that we learn in our classes every day.

(24) How can Jackson High make sure that students dress appropriately if it doesn't have a dress code? (25) That's what some teachers have said to me. (26) I think the answer is obvious. (27) Teach us, the students, how people are suppossed to dress in the real world when they have jobs. (28) Explain why certain choices might be inappropriate. (29) Than let us make our own decisions. (30) That's what we learn in all our classes, and that's how it should be for the dress code.

32. What is the most effective way to rewrite sentence 2?

a. Some of the outfits students wear to school, she is saying, are distracting and not appropriate.
b. The outfits are distracting and inappropriate, she says, that students wear to school.
c. She says that some of the outfits that students wear to school are distracting and inappropriate.
d. She says that it is distracting and inappropriate that students wear outfits to school.

33. What change, if any, should be made to sentence 7?

a. Change *your* to *you're*
b. Insert a comma before *and*
c. Change *about* to *on*
d. No change

34. What is the most effective way to combine sentences 11 and 12?

a. A lot of teens express themselves through fashion, and since many teens start earning their own money, they can buy their own clothes and choose the fashions that they want.
b. A lot of teens express themselves through fashion and since many teens start earning their own money, they can buy their own clothes and choose the fashions that they want.
c. A lot of teens express themselves through fashion, but since many teens start earning their own money, they can buy their own clothes and choose the fashions that they want.
d. A lot of teens express themselves through fashion but since many teens start earning their own money, they can buy their own clothes and choose the fashions that they want.

35. What change should be made to sentence 13?

a. Change *if* to *because*
b. Add a comma after *code*
c. Change *students* to *students'*
d. Change *themselves* to *theirselves*

36. What change should be made in sentence 14?

a. Change *expression* to *expresion*
b. Insert a comma before *and*
c. Change *are* to *is*
d. Insert *the* after *at*

37. What transition should be added to the beginning of sentence 18?

a. However
b. Furthermore
c. First of all
d. Therefore

38. What change should be made to sentence 22?

a. Change *however* to *nevertheless*
b. Change ***a** couple* to *several*
c. Change *teacher's* to *teachers*
d. Delete the comma after ***code***

39. What change should be made in sentence 27?

a. Delete the comma after *us*
b. Change *suppossed* to *supposed*
c. Change *real world* to *real-world*
d. Change *jobs* to *job's*

40. What change, if any, should be made to sentence 28?

a. Change *explain* to *explaining*
b. Insert *not* after *might*
c. Change *inappropriate* to *inapropriate*
d. No change

41. What change should be made in sentence 29?

a. Change *than* to *then*
b. Insert *you* before *let*
c. Insert *to* after *us*
d. Change *decisions* to *descisions*

Revising and Editing Text 2

Questions 42 – 51 pertain to the following:

Jordan's English class is reading a book set in the 1920s. In order to better understand that decade, his English teacher has assigned a research essay on one aspect of that time period. Jordan has written an essay on early pilots but needs help revising and improving the essay. After you read the essay, answer the questions that follow.

(1) After Orville and Wilbur Wright have flown their first airplane in 1903, the age of flying slowly began. (2) Many new pilots learned how to fly in World War I, which the United States joined in 1917. (3) During the war, the American public loved hearing stories about the daring pilots and their air fights. (4) But after the war ended, many Americans thought that men and women belonged on the ground and not in the air.

(5) In the years after the war and through the Roaring Twenties, Americas pilots found themselves without jobs. (6) Some of them gave up flying altogether. (7) Pilot Eddie Rickenbacker, who used to be called America's Ace of Aces, became a car salesman. (8) But other pilots found new and creative things to do with their airplanes.

(9) Pilot Casey Jones used his airplane to help get news across the country. (10) When a big news story broke, Jones flew news photos to newspapers in different cities. (11) Another pilot, Roscoe Turner traveled around the country with a lion cub in his plane. (12) The cub was the mascot of an oil company, and Turner convinced the company that flying the cub around would be a good advertisement. (13) The Humane Society wasn't very happy about this idea, and they convinced Turner to make sure the lion cub always wore a parachute.

(14) Other pilots took people for short airplane rides, often charging five dollars for a five-minute ride (by comparison, you could buy a loaf of bread for about ten cents in 1920). (15) These pilots, called barnstormers, often used dangerous tricks to get customers: two barnstormers once stood on a plane's wings and played tennis while the plane flew at 70 miles per hour! (16) Many barnstormers advertised their shows as a 'flying circus.'

(17) During the 1920s, the US Post Office developed airmail. (18) Before airmail, the post traveled on trains and can take weeks to reach a destination. (19) Flying for the post office was dangerous work. (20) Early pilots didn't have sophistocated instruments and safety equipment on their planes. (21) Many of them had to bail out and use their parachutes when their planes iced up in the cold air or had other trouble.

(22) The most famous pilot of the 1920s, Charles A. Lindbergh, began as a postal pilot. (23) In May 1927, he participated in an air race to fly across the Atlantic Ocean. (24) The prize was $25,000, but the dangers were extensive. (25) Named Nungesser and Coli, two French pilots had recently tried to fly across the Atlantic. (26) They disappeared.

(27) The newspapers called Charles Lindbergh "the dark horse" to win the race. (28) He had already set a record by making the fastest solo flight between St. Louis, Missouri, and, San Diego, California. (29) Lindbergh's record-setting flight took 23 hours and 15 minutes; today, a flight between St. Louis and San Diego takes about four hours.

(30) After several weather delays, Lindbergh took off in his small plane, The Spirit of St. Louis, on May 20, 1927. (31) He made it across the Atlantic Ocean and arrived in France after 33 hours and 30 minutes of non-stop flight; today, a flight from New York to Paris would take about seven hours.

(32) The flight was taxing. (33) Because Lindbergh flew alone, he had to stay awake for the entire trip. (34) He knew that he couldn't have made it across without a great plane. (35) He said, "I feel that the monoplane was as much a part of the trip as myself."

(36) Lindbergh's trip set off a golden age for aviation. (37) The same people who were nervous about airplanes at the beginning of the 1920s came out by the thousands to

cheer Lindbergh. (38) The age of pilots doing odd jobs and dangerous stunt work had ended.

42. What change should be made to sentence 1?

a. Add a comma after *Wright*
b. Change *have flown* to *flew*
c. Change *first* to *1st*
d. Delete the comma after *1903*

43. What change should be made to sentence 5?

a. Change *years* to *year's*
b. Delete the comma after *Twenties*
c. Change *Americas* to *America's*
d. Change *themselves* to *theirselves*

44. What change should be made in sentence 11?

a. Delete the comma before *Roscoe*
b. Add a comma after *Turner*
c. Change *with* to *as*
d. Change *plane* to *airplane*

45. What change should be made to sentence 15?

a. Change *barnstormers* to *barnstormer*
b. Change the colon after *customers* to a semicolon
c. Change *plane's* to *planes*
d. Change *while* to *when*

46. What change should be made to sentence 18?

a. Delete the comma after *airmail*
b. Change *traveled* to *travelled*
c. Change *can* to *could*
d. Change *a* to *it's*

47. What change should be made to sentence 20?

a. Change *pilots* to *pilot's*
b. Change *sophistocated* to *sophisticated*
c. Add a comma after *instruments*
d. Change *their* to *they're*

48. What's the most effective way to rewrite sentence 25?

a. Two French pilots, named Nungesser and Coli, had recently tried to fly across the Atlantic.
b. Two French pilots Nungesser and Coli had recently tried to fly across the Atlantic.
c. Recently having tried to fly across the Atlantic, two French pilots were named Nungesser and Coli.
d. No change

49. What change should be made to sentence 28?

a. Delete the comma after *St. Louis*
b. Delete the comma after *Missouri*
c. Delete the comma after *and*
d. Delete the comma after *San Diego*

50. How could sentences 34 and 35 best be combined?

a. He knew that he couldn't have made it across without a great plane and he said, "I feel that the monoplane was as much a part of the trip as myself."
b. He knew that he couldn't have made it across without a great plane, he said, "I feel that the monoplane was as much a part of the trip as myself."
c. He knew that he couldn't have made it across without a great plane and says, "I feel that the monoplane was as much a part of the trip as myself."
d. He knew that he couldn't have made it across without a great plane and said, "I feel that the monoplane was as much a part of the trip as myself."

51. What transition could be added at the beginning of sentence 36?

a. In conclusion
b. Furthermore
c. Therefore
d. Additionally

WRITTEN COMPOSITION

Write an essay about a time you experienced something new.

Answers and Explanations

1. A: because the passage says that Alice is 'burning with curiosity.' This means that Alice feels an intense curiosity about the White Rabbit. The other three choices are incorrect because they are referring to temperature or fire rather than the intensity of Alice's curiosity.

2. B: because Alice is feeling bored with sitting by her sister and doing nothing, she feels eager to follow the White Rabbit once he appears. Although the first sentence of paragraph 1 says Alice is getting tired, the word 'tired' is not referring to sleepiness, which makes choice A incorrect. Choice C is incorrect because Alice only feels curious after she sees the White Rabbit. The setting, however, makes her feel bored and restless. Choice D is incorrect because Alice says she doesn't feel like reading because her sister's book does not have pictures.

3. D: because Alice says that she has no idea what the words mean but that she thinks they are nice, big words. Choice A is incorrect because, although latitude and longitude can help people find locations on a map, Alice does not know what the words mean. Even though Alice says the words because they're big and impressive, choice B is incorrect because Alice has no one to show off to; she's alone in the rabbit hole. Choice C is incorrect because Alice does not listen for an echo or comment on hearing one.

4. B: is correct because the words are capitalized to emphasize the absurdity of Alice's situation. Choice A is incorrect because this passage is a finished, published excerpt that has already been proofread. Choice C is incorrect because Alice's demeanor shows that she is not upset by falling; in fact, she's intrigued by her new situation. Choice D is incorrect because there is no one else in the rabbit hole that Alice could talk to.

5. A: because Alice examines the bottle and tries to determine if it is poison. Choices B, C, and D are incorrect because Alice is not showing extreme emotion. Instead, she looks at the bottle very analytically and thinks carefully about whether or not she should drink from it.

6. C: the correct answer because Alice is worried that she will continue shrinking and go "out altogether, like a candle." Choice A is incorrect because Alice has already determined that the bottle is not poison. Choice B is incorrect because Alice and the reader have already seen proof that the liquid is working because Alice is getting smaller. Although Alice uses a flame analogy to explain her fears about shrinking forever, choice D is incorrect because Alice is not actually worried about turning into a flame.

7. D: is the correct answer because details from paragraphs 6-10, such as the extraordinarily long rabbit hole and the cupboards on the walls, show that the story is going to be fantasy. Because it is clear from these details that the story will contain elements that are not real, choice C is incorrect. Although falling through a rabbit hole might seem like a dangerous situation, choice A is incorrect because the passage doesn't convey any sense of urgency or danger. Instead, Alice is experiencing a leisurely fall through the rabbit hole. Choice B is incorrect because Alice portrays curiosity rather than nervousness.

8. B: because the key only opens a very small door that Alice can't fit through. Choice A is incorrect because the text says that Alice uses the key to open one of the doors. Choice C is incorrect because Alice doesn't start shrinking until paragraph 18, after she drinks the liquid. Choice D is incorrect because Alice has been in a strange, unknown setting for most of the passage, not just in this paragraph.

9. C: Although there are many unusual things about the rabbit, choice C is correct because the author uses capitalization to show the unusualness of the rabbit's watch. Choice A is incorrect because the text says that there is nothing very remarkable in the pink eyes. Choice B is also incorrect because the text says that Alice doesn't think it is that unusual to hear the rabbit speak. Choice D is incorrect because Alice might expect a rabbit to go into a rabbit hole.

10. B: is correct because the fall through the rabbit hole is so long that any future fall, even one down the stairs, will seem like nothing. Choice A is incorrect because Alice hasn't discovered any methods for falling. Choice C is incorrect because Alice is not mentioning clumsiness. Although Alice says that her family will think she's brave if she falls down the stairs without getting upset, choice D is incorrect because Alice's main thought is that any future falls will be less extreme than this fall down the rabbit hole.

11. A: because Alice goes down the rabbit hole without even thinking about how she will get out. Choice B, that Alice is thoughtful, is the opposite of impulsive and is incorrect because Alice doesn't think about consequences before she goes down the rabbit hole. Although Alice is curious, choice C is incorrect because the previous paragraphs have already established Alice's curiosity. Choice D is incorrect because Alice is not sneaking around; she's simply following the rabbit because it intrigues her.

12. B: because the narrator says that she and Ed decided to have breakfast at Café A. She also says that she has never seen a worse breakfast. Although she drinks a cup of English Breakfast tea, choice A is not correct because the tea is only one part of the breakfast. Choice C is not correct because they buy the peppermints after they eat the breakfast, or repast. Although the narrator says she pities the subjects of King Edward (the King of England) if they have to drink the awful tea frequently, "repast" isn't referring to the King because it is something that is eaten.

13. C: because the narrator says that she is taking a boat along the St. Lawrence and comments on the huge castles and small cottages that she sees along the way. Choice A is incorrect because the narrator announces at the beginning of paragraph 3 that she has left the United States. Although the narrator mentions the Rhine River in paragraph 4, she is not on the Rhine yet. She's planning on journeying down the Rhine at a later date and says that she'll be disappointed if it is not more entrancing than the St. Lawrence. Choice D is incorrect because, although the narrator and Ed joke at the image of children playing in the river, they don't actually see any children.

14: A: is correct because the narrator comments in paragraph 5 that "the castles are too new, the homes do not show the caress of time..." Choice B is incorrect because she wishes that the cottages and castles were older and is displeased that they are not. Choice C is incorrect because, although the narrator mentions that the Thousand Islands have 1,642 islands, she does not express anger about it. Choice D is incorrect because the narrator does not actually see any children playing while she sails through the Thousand Islands, she only imagines them playing in the river.

15. C: Although the narrator traveled all over Montreal, the best answer is choice C, when she views the city from up high on Mount Royal. She says in paragraph 13 that she is able to learn Montreal fairly well after looking at the city and listening to Ed describe all the buildings. Choice A is incorrect because the narrator sails through the Thousand Islands before arriving in Montreal. Although the narrator does eat at Café A, which is in Montreal, choice B is incorrect because the café is only one building in the entire city. Choice D is incorrect because Madame K. gives the narrator a tour of Convent of the Ladies of the Sacred Heart, not Montreal.

16. D: is correct because the sentence indicates that Ed is remembering breakfasts from his childhood. He liked the food at Café A as a child and thought, incorrectly, that it would be just as delicious when he was an adult. Choice A is incorrect because it indicates that the breakfast tasted bad but doesn't explain the reason why Ed thought the breakfast would taste good. Choice B is incorrect because the narrator feels sorry for King Edward's subjects if they're forced to drink English Breakfast tea every morning. Choice C is incorrect because the narrator is talking about the pastry that she ate after the terrible breakfast at Café A.

17. D: because the narrator is describing her visit to Montreal through a letter to her mother. If the narrator wanted to write a travel book, as in choice A, she would have needed to describe the sites she saw in more detail. Instead, she talked more about her experiences. Choice B is incorrect because the narrator's purpose in writing is to describe her visit, which is already in progress. Although the narrator does meet with a teacher from her childhood, choice C is incorrect because the primary purpose is to describe the entire day in Montreal.

18. C: because the narrator is making a joke that it may not have been pleasurable to teach Ed. The reader can determine that it's a joke because the narrator shows affection for Ed throughout the passage. Choice A is incorrect because the narrator does not give any indication that she's worried about the word's spelling. Choice B is incorrect because the narrator does not give her opinion about the priest. Choice D is incorrect because the narrator knows for a fact that the priest taught Ed.

19. A: because the narrator displays her enthusiasm for traveling through her detailed descriptions of the day. Although the narrator is irritated about some aspects of her day, such as the breakfast at Café A, choice B is incorrect because she is enjoying her overall experience. Choice C is incorrect because the narrator does not indicate that she wishes to go see her mother; instead, she shares her experiences with her mother by writing the letter. Choice D is incorrect because, while the narrator may be looking forward to seeing Quebec, she does not indicate that she is impatient to leave Montreal.

20. B: is the correct answer because the narrator describes some of Ed's childhood experiences, such as his meals at Café A and his schooling. These experiences indicate that he grew up in Montreal. Choice A is incorrect because it is clear that Ed has been in Montreal before. Choice C is incorrect because the narrator uses words such as "wondrous" (paragraph 13) to describe Montreal, which indicates that she does not dislike Montreal. Finally, choice D is incorrect because the narrator is not familiar with Montreal and relies on Ed to tell her about the city.

21. C: is correct because the narrator jokes that even though the Great Spirit initially wanted to punish the man, the Spirit would have to save the man if he came across the Lachine Rapids. Choice A is incorrect because the narrator does not display any signs of homesickness; instead, she shows that she is eager to continue exploring Montreal. Choice B is incorrect because the narrator is not comparing the main character from the legend to the rapids; instead, she is imagining how his story would have changed if he saw the rapids. Choice D is incorrect because the rapids remind the narrator of the story, not the fallen bridge.

22. A: Although the narrator does not define the word *presidents*, choice A is correct because it is clear that they are pastries when the narrator buys them in a bakery and then says that the pastry was delicious. Choice B is incorrect because the narrator is talking about something that she's eating. Although Ed was dreaming of the peppermints since childhood, choice C is incorrect because the narrator is actually experiencing the pastries. Choice D is incorrect because the narrator is referring to pastries, not to the bakery where she bought them.

23. B: is the correct answer because both passages are about exploration. In *Letters from an Oklahoman*, the narrator is exploring a new a city, and in *Alice's Adventures in Wonderland*, Alice is discovering a new world. Choice A is incorrect because only the narrator from *Letters* is traveling with a companion (Ed), while Alice is alone in the excerpt. Choice C is incorrect because, although Alice sees a fantastical thing (the talking rabbit with a stopwatch), the narrator from *Letters* doesn't see anything that she believes to be magic. Choice D is incorrect because only the narrator from *Letters* travels by boat; Alice travels by falling down the rabbit hole.

24. A: because both the narrator from *Letters from an Oklahoman* and Alice show curiosity at their new surroundings. The narrator from *Letters* shows curiosity by exploring the different parts of Montreal, and Alice shows curiosity by looking in the cabinets as she falls. While the reader might expect Alice to feel fear as she's falling, she is calm and curious instead, which makes choice B incorrect. The narrator from *Letters* also does not show fear. Choice C is incorrect because only the narrator from *Letters* shows disappointment in the reading excerpts. She has several small moments of disappointment, including after the breakfast at Café A. Choice D is incorrect because only the narrator from *Letters* shows any excitement about her surroundings. The reader might expect Alice to show excitement about her adventure, but she is very calm about her experience.

25. D: because both the narrator from *Letters from an Oklahoman* and Alice are embarking on a journey. Choice A is incorrect because only *Alice's Adventures in Wonderland* contains unique animals. The narrator from *Letters* discusses some of Ed's memories, but choice B is incorrect because Alice doesn't think of any memories. Choice C is incorrect because only the narrator from *Letters* sees historic buildings.

26. C: because all of the items on the list could be used on a mountain. A windbreaker or down jacket could be used when the weather is poor, hiking boots could be used to go for a hike, and shorts could be used in warm weather. Choice A is incorrect because rainforests are not known for cold climates. Choice B is incorrect because it doesn't rain frequently in the desert. Choice D is incorrect because it doesn't typically get cold enough for a down jacket on a tropical beach.

27. B: because it's logical to assume that Aisha is packing the items she thinks she'll need. She may be packing more short-sleeve shirts because she expects to wear them more often. While she may be worried that some of the short sleeve shirts will get lost, choice A is a less logical choice because if Aisha is worried about losing one type of shirt, she's likely worried about both. While it's possible that Aisha only has five long sleeve shirts, choice C is incorrect because it's more logical that Aisha expects to wear the short sleeve shirts more frequently. Choice D is incorrect because there is no indication on the list that Aisha is running out of room in her suitcase.

28. A: is the most logical answer because Aisha is clearly going to be spending time outside. The reader can determine this because of the hiking boots, down jacket, and rain slicker on her list. Like those items, a hat will help her protect herself from the elements. Choice B is incorrect because a skirt doesn't fit in with the other items on the list, and would not be a logical choice for a trip that involves hiking and outdoor time. While Aisha might want to wear sandals with her shorts, choice C is incorrect because she's clearly planning to spend time in a rugged terrain where sandals might be dangerous. Choice D is incorrect because she already has two jackets; a wool coat is not the most logical choice if she needs one more item.

29. Sample Answer:

The author does not directly tell the reader about Alice's personality, but he indirectly shows her personality in several places. For example, at the beginning of the passage, the reader learns that Alice gets bored easily and doesn't like sitting around with nothing to do. The author doesn't say this outright, but he shows how Alice doesn't want to sit around with her sister. The author also shows Alice's curiosity by showing her exploring the cabinets in the rabbit hole. He never says that she's curious, but the reader can infer that Alice is a curious person by observing her actions.

30. Sample Answer:

The narrator of "Letters from an Oklahoman Abroad" shows enthusiasm for her trip throughout the passage. It is clear that she enjoys seeing new places, such as when she says in paragraph 14, "The trolley ride was so cool and through such fine country I was rather sorry when the convent cross appeared." In this sentence, the narrator is expressing her enjoyment of her trip. Even when she is unhappy, she maintains an optimistic tone that shows she is looking forward to future travels. For example, in paragraph 4 she says that she's disappointed that the houses in the Thousand Islands looked too new. However, she then says that she hopes the castles on the Rhine, which she will visit later in her travels, have that old quality. This sentence shows that she's looking forward to more travels and not yet ready to go home.

31. Sample Answer:

While both Alice and the narrator from "Letters from an Oklahoman Abroad" have adventurous spirits, I think Alice is more adventurous. Alice thrusts herself into the unknown by jumping into the rabbit hole all by herself. She takes another risk when she drinks the strange liquid. The narrator from "Letters from an Oklahoman Abroad" is also adventurous, but she seems less so because she is traveling in comfort and safety. For example, she knows where she is going to sleep at night (the hotel in paragraph 7) whereas Alice doesn't even know how or if she will ever get home. Alice is also traveling all alone while the narrator from "Letters" is traveling with her husband and has guides.

32. C: because this version begins with a subject and verb and is followed by a clause. Choice A is incorrect because the words are out of order and don't logically follow the previous sentence. Sentence 2 should begin with 'She says' because it is the school principal's opinion being expressed. This choice is also incorrect because it uses the words *not appropriate* instead of *inappropriate*. Choice B is incorrect because the clause "that students wear to schools" should come after the word *outfits*. Choice D is incorrect because the word order changes the meaning of the sentence by stating that any outfits are distracting and inappropriate.

33. A: is correct because *your* is the possessive of *you* while *you're* is a conjunction that stands for *you are*. Because it makes sense to substitute *you are* for *you're*, choice A is correct. Choice B is incorrect because a comma is only required before *and* if it is concluding a series of three or more items. Choice C is incorrect because it is correct to write *learn about* but incorrect to write *learn on*. Choice D is incorrect because *your* should be written as the conjunction *you're*.

34. A: because it uses correct punctuation and a logical conjunction. Because the conjunction *and* connects two independent clauses (meaning that they can stand on their own as sentences), there must be a comma before the conjunction. Therefore, choices B and D are incorrect because they are missing this comma. While choice C does have a comma before the conjunction, it uses the conjunction *but* rather than *and*. *But* implies that the two clauses contradict each other. *And* is a better choice because the two clauses are connected and support each other.

35. B: is correct because the phrase *If Jackson high adopts a dress code* is a dependent clause that is followed by an independent clause. Because there is no conjunction, these two clauses must be separated by a comma. Choice A is incorrect because the word *because* would only be used if the dress code had already been adopted. Choice C is incorrect because *students'* would require the word to be a possessive, even though the sentence does not show the students possessing anything. Choice D is incorrect because *theirselves* is not a real word.

36. C: because the verb *are* does not match the subject, *self expression*, which is singular. Choice A is incorrect because *expression* is already written with the correct spelling. Choice B is incorrect because the conjunction *and* is connecting an independent clause with a dependent clause. When *and* is used in this way, there should not be a comma before the conjunction. Choice D is incorrect because an article is not needed before the name of the school, which is a proper noun.

37. B: is correct because the word *furthermore* shows that the sentence will present additional support for the writer's argument. Choice A is incorrect because *however* indicates that the following sentence will contradict what came before. Choice C is incorrect because the sentence is not presenting the first point in the writer's argument. Choice D is incorrect because the sentence is not presenting a conclusion, but an additional point.

38. C: because *teacher's* is not being used as a possessive. Instead, it's being used as a plural noun and therefore should not have an apostrophe. Choice A is incorrect because *however* is a better transition to sentence 22 due to the sentence showing a contrast with a previous point. Choice B is incorrect because the word *of* should not follow *several*. Choice D is incorrect because the comma correctly separates a dependent clause from an independent clause.

39. B: is correct because the correct spelling of the word only has a single *s*. Choice A is incorrect because the comma is required to set off the non-essential clause *the students*. Choice C is incorrect because *real* is an adjective modifying *world*, and it is incorrect to put a hyphen in between an adjective and a noun. Choice D is incorrect because *jobs* is a plural noun, not a possessive.

40. D: is correct because the sentence does not have any errors. Choice A is incorrect because sentences should not begin with a declarative verb. Choice B is incorrect because *not* changes the meaning of the sentence to the opposite of the writer's point. Choice C is incorrect because *inappropriate* is spelled correctly.

41. A: because *than* is a comparison word while *then* indicates a conclusion. Choice B is incorrect because *you* indicates that the writer is addressing a specific person, which is not the case. Choice D is incorrect because *decisions* is already written with the correct spelling.

42. B: is the correct answer because the verb should be in past tense rather than present tense. Choice A is incorrect because a comma should not separate the subject and verb of a sentence. Choice C is incorrect because it is better to write out *first* than it is to use numerical digits. Choice D is incorrect because a comma is required to separate the dependent clause at the beginning of the sentence from the independent clause at the end of the sentence.

43. C: because *America's* is possessive. The sentence is referring to the pilots who lived in America. Choice A is incorrect because *years* is plural and not possessive. Choice B is incorrect because the comma correctly separates the dependent clause at the beginning of the sentence from the independent clause at the end of the sentence. Choice D is incorrect because *theirselves* is not a real word.

44. B: is correct because a comma is needed to offset the non-essential clause *Roscoe Turner*. Choice A is incorrect because *Roscoe Turner* is a non-essential clause; it is not required to understand the meaning of the sentence. The clause should be offset by commas on both sides. Choice C is incorrect because *as* would change the meaning of the sentence to imply that Roscoe Turner dressed as a lion cub. Choice D is incorrect because the words *plane* and *airplane* can be used interchangeably.

45. B: because a semicolon is used to separate two related independent clauses. In contrast, a colon is used to set off lists. Choice A is incorrect because *barnstormers* is referring to multiple pilots and should remain in the plural. Choice C is incorrect because *plane's* is correctly written as a possessive. Choice D is incorrect because *while* implies that the barnstormers played tennis at the same time as the plane flew.

46. C: is correct because the passage is discussing the past. Therefore, the past tense *could* is preferable over the present tense *can*. Choice A is incorrect because the comma is needed to set off the phrase at the beginning of the sentence. Choice B is incorrect because *traveled* only has a single *l*. Although both *a* and *its* could be used in this sentence, choice D is incorrect because *it's* is a conjunction for *it is* and would be incorrect if used in this part of the sentence.

47. B: because *sophisticated* is the correct spelling. Choice A is incorrect because *pilots* is not a possessive in this context. Choice C is incorrect because a comma is not needed to separate a list that only has two items. Choice D is incorrect because *their* is a possessive, which fits the sentence. *They're* refers to *they are*, which does not work in this sentence.

48. A: is correct because this word order best conveys the meaning of the sentence in a concise manner. Choice B is incorrect because *Nungesser and Coli* is a non-essential phrase and needs to be separated from the rest of the sentence with commas. Choice C inverts the order to the sentence and makes it more awkward; it is better to have a simple subject and verb at the beginning of a sentence. Choice D is incorrect because the word order confuses the sentence's meaning.

49. B: because a comma is rarely needed after the word *and*. A comma would only be required if a non-essential phrase followed *and*. However, the word *and* in this sentence simply separates a two-item series. The other commas are correct because commas should be used both before and after a state's name.

50. D: is correct because it uses the correct punctuation and verb tense. Choice A is incorrect because the conjunction *and* separates two independent clauses; when the conjunction is used in this way, a comma must come before it. Choice B is incorrect because there is no conjunction between the two independent clauses, making the answer choice a run-on sentence. Choice C is incorrect because the passage is written in the past tense but *says* is incorrectly written in the present tense.

51. A: is the best answer choice because *in conclusion* sums up the essay and leads into the final paragraph. Choices B and D are incorrect because the words *furthermore* and *additionally* indicate that an additional argument will be made. However, sentence 35 begins a concluding paragraph. Choice C is incorrect because the word *therefore* should be used as a conclusion to a specific point rather than the conclusion of an entire essay.

Sample Written Composition:

On my first day of high school, I didn't experience as many new things as the narrator of "Letters from an Oklahoman Abroad" or Alice in "Alice's Adventures in Wonderland," but I still felt like I was stepping into a whole new world. My high school was a big, brick building in the center of town. I passed it lots of times when I was a kid, but I only went inside on a couple of school field trips. The building looked familiar on the outside but was a strange mystery on the inside. How would I ever find my classes? Could I find any friends in the thousands of people? I was scared and excited the summer before my freshman year, which may be how the narrator from "Letters" felt the night before her big trip started.

Two days before the first day of school, three of my middle school friends and I got our schedules and found all of our new classes. When we first started walking around, I felt incredibly confused. Hallways seemed to shoot off in all directions, and there were A, B, C, and D wings that I knew I could never keep straight. But as my friends and I walked our schedules again and again, the maze of hallways started to make sense. The A hall was connected through the B hall, and if you walked through the outdoor courtyard, you could take a shortcut to the D hall. Slowly, the halls of the high school became more familiar, just as Montreal became more familiar to the narrator of "Letters."

On the first day of school, I felt nervous and excited. I took the bus, and it was filled with familiar faces from middle school. But when the bus dropped us off, I was suddenly surrounded by hundreds of people I didn't know. I felt like running away, but I followed everyone inside and made my way to my first class. Inside, the halls were filled with unfamiliar faces. Most of the people were taller than me, and they were all pushing, laughing, or hurrying past. I had thought that I could do it, but at that moment, I just wanted to go back to eighth grade. Just when I was ready to go into the bathroom and be sick, I saw a familiar face, a girl I knew from middle school. May and I weren't friends in middle school – we barely ever talked – but when we saw each other, we both smiled. Suddenly, in the middle of this huge, terrifying high school, I felt a little bit at home.

After that first day of school, I realized that I have a lot of new things to experience in my life. I was scared when I went to get my driver's license last month, and I'm already nervous for SATs next year. But seeing May in the crowded hall on the first day of school helped me realize that a little bit of the familiar makes it easier to get through brand new experiences.

How to Overcome Test Anxiety

Just the thought of taking a test is enough to make most people a little nervous. A test is an important event that can have a long-term impact on your future, so it's important to take it seriously and it's natural to feel anxious about performing well. But just because anxiety is normal, that doesn't mean that it's helpful in test taking, or that you should simply accept it as part of your life. Anxiety can have a variety of effects. These effects can be mild, like making you feel slightly nervous, or severe, like blocking your ability to focus or remember even a simple detail.

If you experience test anxiety—whether severe or mild—it's important to know how to beat it. To discover this, first you need to understand what causes test anxiety.

Causes of Test Anxiety

While we often think of anxiety as an uncontrollable emotional state, it can actually be caused by simple, practical things. One of the most common causes of test anxiety is that a person does not feel adequately prepared for their test. This feeling can be the result of many different issues such as poor study habits or lack of organization, but the most common culprit is time management. Starting to study too late, failing to organize your study time to cover all of the material, or being distracted while you study will mean that you're not well prepared for the test. This may lead to cramming the night before, which will cause you to be physically and mentally exhausted for the test. Poor time management also contributes to feelings of stress, fear, and hopelessness as you realize you are not well prepared but don't know what to do about it.

Other times, test anxiety is not related to your preparation for the test but comes from unresolved fear. This may be a past failure on a test, or poor performance on tests in general. It may come from comparing yourself to others who seem to be performing better or from the stress of living up to expectations. Anxiety may be driven by fears of the future—how failure on this test would affect your educational and career goals. These fears are often completely irrational, but they can still negatively impact your test performance.

Elements of Test Anxiety

As mentioned earlier, test anxiety is considered to be an emotional state, but it has physical and mental components as well. Sometimes you may not even realize that you are suffering from test anxiety until you notice the physical symptoms. These can include trembling hands, rapid heartbeat, sweating, nausea, and tense muscles. Extreme anxiety may lead to fainting or vomiting. Obviously, any of these symptoms can have a negative impact on testing. It is important to recognize them as soon as they begin to occur so that you can address the problem before it damages your performance.

The mental components of test anxiety include trouble focusing and inability to remember learned information. During a test, your mind is on high alert, which can help you recall information and stay focused for an extended period of time. However, anxiety interferes with your mind's natural processes, causing you to blank out, even on the questions you know well. The strain of testing during anxiety makes it difficult to stay focused, especially on a test that may take several hours. Extreme anxiety can take a huge mental toll, making it difficult not only to recall test information but even to understand the test questions or pull your thoughts together.

Effects of Test Anxiety

Test anxiety is like a disease—if left untreated, it will get progressively worse. Anxiety leads to poor performance, and this reinforces the feelings of fear and failure, which in turn lead to poor performances on subsequent tests. It can grow from a mild nervousness to a crippling condition. If allowed to progress, test anxiety can have a big impact on your schooling, and consequently on your future.

Test anxiety can spread to other parts of your life. Anxiety on tests can become anxiety in any stressful situation, and blanking on a test can turn into panicking in a job situation. But fortunately, you don't have to let anxiety rule your testing and determine your grades. There are a number of relatively simple steps you can take to move past anxiety and function normally on a test and in the rest of life.

Physical Steps for Beating Test Anxiety

While test anxiety is a serious problem, the good news is that it can be overcome. It doesn't have to control your ability to think and remember information. While it may take time, you can begin taking steps today to beat anxiety.

Just as your first hint that you may be struggling with anxiety comes from the physical symptoms, the first step to treating it is also physical. Rest is crucial for having a clear, strong mind. If you are tired, it is much easier to give in to anxiety. But if you establish good sleep habits, your body and mind will be ready to perform optimally, without the strain of exhaustion. Additionally, sleeping well helps you to retain information better, so you're more likely to recall the answers when you see the test questions.

Getting good sleep means more than going to bed on time. It's important to allow your brain time to relax. Take study breaks from time to time so it doesn't get overworked, and don't study right before bed. Take time to rest your mind before trying to rest your body, or you may find it difficult to fall asleep.

Along with sleep, other aspects of physical health are important in preparing for a test. Good nutrition is vital for good brain function. Sugary foods and drinks may give a burst of energy but this burst is followed by a crash, both physically and emotionally. Instead, fuel your body with protein and vitamin-rich foods.

Also, drink plenty of water. Dehydration can lead to headaches and exhaustion, especially if your brain is already under stress from the rigors of the test. Particularly if your test is a long one, drink water during the breaks. And if possible, take an energy-boosting snack to eat between sections.

Along with sleep and diet, a third important part of physical health is exercise. Maintaining a steady workout schedule is helpful, but even taking 5-minute study breaks to walk can help get your blood pumping faster and clear your head. Exercise also releases endorphins, which contribute to a positive feeling and can help combat test anxiety.

When you nurture your physical health, you are also contributing to your mental health. If your body is healthy, your mind is much more likely to be healthy as well. So take time to rest, nourish your body with healthy food and water, and get moving as much as possible. Taking these physical steps will make you stronger and more able to take the mental steps necessary to overcome test anxiety.

Mental Steps for Beating Test Anxiety

Working on the mental side of test anxiety can be more challenging, but as with the physical side, there are clear steps you can take to overcome it. As mentioned earlier, test anxiety often stems from lack of preparation, so the obvious solution is to prepare for the test. Effective studying may be the most important weapon you have for beating test anxiety, but you can and should employ several other mental tools to combat fear.

First, boost your confidence by reminding yourself of past success—tests or projects that you aced. If you're putting as much effort into preparing for this test as you did for those, there's no reason you should expect to fail here. Work hard to prepare; then trust your preparation.

Second, surround yourself with encouraging people. It can be helpful to find a study group, but be sure that the people you're around will encourage a positive attitude. If you spend time with others who are anxious or cynical, this will only contribute to your own anxiety. Look for others who are motivated to study hard from a desire to succeed, not from a fear of failure.

Third, reward yourself. A test is physically and mentally tiring, even without anxiety, and it can be helpful to have something to look forward to. Plan an activity following the test, regardless of the outcome, such as going to a movie or getting ice cream.

When you are taking the test, if you find yourself beginning to feel anxious, remind yourself that you know the material. Visualize successfully completing the test. Then take a few deep, relaxing breaths and return to it. Work through the questions carefully but with confidence, knowing that you are capable of succeeding.

Developing a healthy mental approach to test taking will also aid in other areas of life. Test anxiety affects more than just the actual test—it can be damaging to your mental health and even contribute to depression. It's important to beat test anxiety before it becomes a problem for more than testing.

Study Strategy

Being prepared for the test is necessary to combat anxiety, but what does being prepared look like? You may study for hours on end and still not feel prepared. What you need is a strategy for test prep. The next few pages outline our recommended steps to help you plan out and conquer the challenge of preparation.

Step 1: Scope Out the Test

Learn everything you can about the format (multiple choice, essay, etc.) and what will be on the test. Gather any study materials, course outlines, or sample exams that may be available. Not only will this help you to prepare, but knowing what to expect can help to alleviate test anxiety.

Step 2: Map Out the Material

Look through the textbook or study guide and make note of how many chapters or sections it has. Then divide these over the time you have. For example, if a book has 15 chapters and you have five days to study, you need to cover three chapters each day. Even better, if you have the time, leave an extra day at the end for overall review after you have gone through the material in depth.

If time is limited, you may need to prioritize the material. Look through it and make note of which sections you think you already have a good grasp on, and which need review. While you are studying, skim quickly through the familiar sections and take more time on the challenging parts.

Write out your plan so you don't get lost as you go. Having a written plan also helps you feel more in control of the study, so anxiety is less likely to arise from feeling overwhelmed at the amount to cover.

STEP 3: GATHER YOUR TOOLS

Decide what study method works best for you. Do you prefer to highlight in the book as you study and then go back over the highlighted portions? Or do you type out notes of the important information? Or is it helpful to make flashcards that you can carry with you? Assemble the pens, index cards, highlighters, post-it notes, and any other materials you may need so you won't be distracted by getting up to find things while you study.

If you're having a hard time retaining the information or organizing your notes, experiment with different methods. For example, try color-coding by subject with colored pens, highlighters, or post-it notes. If you learn better by hearing, try recording yourself reading your notes so you can listen while in the car, working out, or simply sitting at your desk. Ask a friend to quiz you from your flashcards, or try teaching someone the material to solidify it in your mind.

STEP 4: CREATE YOUR ENVIRONMENT

It's important to avoid distractions while you study. This includes both the obvious distractions like visitors and the subtle distractions like an uncomfortable chair (or a too-comfortable couch that makes you want to fall asleep). Set up the best study environment possible: good lighting and a comfortable work area. If background music helps you focus, you may want to turn it on, but otherwise keep the room quiet. If you are using a computer to take notes, be sure you don't have any other windows open, especially applications like social media, games, or anything else that could distract you. Silence your phone and turn off notifications. Be sure to keep water close by so you stay hydrated while you study (but avoid unhealthy drinks and snacks).

Also, take into account the best time of day to study. Are you freshest first thing in the morning? Try to set aside some time then to work through the material. Is your mind clearer in the afternoon or evening? Schedule your study session then. Another method is to study at the same time of day that you will take the test, so that your brain gets used to working on the material at that time and will be ready to focus at test time.

STEP 5: STUDY!

Once you have done all the study preparation, it's time to settle into the actual studying. Sit down, take a few moments to settle your mind so you can focus, and begin to follow your study plan. Don't give in to distractions or let yourself procrastinate. This is your time to prepare so you'll be ready to fearlessly approach the test. Make the most of the time and stay focused.

Of course, you don't want to burn out. If you study too long you may find that you're not retaining the information very well. Take regular study breaks. For example, taking five minutes out of every hour to walk briskly, breathing deeply and swinging your arms, can help your mind stay fresh.

As you get to the end of each chapter or section, it's a good idea to do a quick review. Remind yourself of what you learned and work on any difficult parts. When you feel that you've mastered the material, move on to the next part. At the end of your study session, briefly skim through your notes again.

But while review is helpful, cramming last minute is NOT. If at all possible, work ahead so that you won't need to fit all your study into the last day. Cramming overloads your brain with more information than it can process and retain, and your tired mind may struggle to recall even previously learned information when it is overwhelmed with last-minute study. Also, the urgent nature of cramming and the stress placed on your brain contribute to anxiety. You'll be more likely to go to the test feeling unprepared and having trouble thinking clearly.

So don't cram, and don't stay up late before the test, even just to review your notes at a leisurely pace. Your brain needs rest more than it needs to go over the information again. In fact, plan to finish your studies by noon or early afternoon the day before the test. Give your brain the rest of the day to relax or focus on other things, and get a good night's sleep. Then you will be fresh for the test and better able to recall what you've studied.

Step 6: Take a Practice Test

Many courses offer sample tests, either online or in the study materials. This is an excellent resource to check whether you have mastered the material, as well as to prepare for the test format and environment.

Check the test format ahead of time: the number of questions, the type (multiple choice, free response, etc.), and the time limit. Then create a plan for working through them. For example, if you have 30 minutes to take a 60-question test, your limit is 30 seconds per question. Spend less time on the questions you know well so that you can take more time on the difficult ones.

If you have time to take several practice tests, take the first one open book, with no time limit. Work through the questions at your own pace and make sure you fully understand them. Gradually work up to taking a test under test conditions: sit at a desk with all study materials put away and set a timer. Pace yourself to make sure you finish the test with time to spare and go back to check your answers if you have time.

After each test, check your answers. On the questions you missed, be sure you understand why you missed them. Did you misread the question (tests can use tricky wording)? Did you forget the information? Or was it something you hadn't learned? Go back and study any shaky areas that the practice tests reveal.

Taking these tests not only helps with your grade, but also aids in combating test anxiety. If you're already used to the test conditions, you're less likely to worry about it, and working through tests until you're scoring well gives you a confidence boost. Go through the practice tests until you feel comfortable, and then you can go into the test knowing that you're ready for it.

Test Tips

On test day, you should be confident, knowing that you've prepared well and are ready to answer the questions. But aside from preparation, there are several test day strategies you can employ to maximize your performance.

First, as stated before, get a good night's sleep the night before the test (and for several nights before that, if possible). Go into the test with a fresh, alert mind rather than staying up late to study.

Try not to change too much about your normal routine on the day of the test. It's important to eat a nutritious breakfast, but if you normally don't eat breakfast at all, consider eating just a protein bar. If you're a coffee drinker, go ahead and have your normal coffee. Just make sure you time it so that the caffeine doesn't wear off right in the middle of your test. Avoid sugary beverages, and drink enough water to stay hydrated but not so much that you need a restroom break 10 minutes into the test. If your test isn't first thing in the morning, consider going for a walk or doing a light workout before the test to get your blood flowing.

Allow yourself enough time to get ready, and leave for the test with plenty of time to spare so you won't have the anxiety of scrambling to arrive in time. Another reason to be early is to select a good seat. It's helpful to sit away from doors and windows, which can be distracting. Find a good seat, get out your supplies, and settle your mind before the test begins.

When the test begins, start by going over the instructions carefully, even if you already know what to expect. Make sure you avoid any careless mistakes by following the directions.

Then begin working through the questions, pacing yourself as you've practiced. If you're not sure on an answer, don't spend too much time on it, and don't let it shake your confidence. Either skip it and come back later, or eliminate as many wrong answers as possible and guess among the remaining ones. Don't dwell on these questions as you continue—put them out of your mind and focus on what lies ahead.

Be sure to read all of the answer choices, even if you're sure the first one is the right answer. Sometimes you'll find a better one if you keep reading. But don't second-guess yourself if you do immediately know the answer. Your gut instinct is usually right. Don't let test anxiety rob you of the information you know.

If you have time at the end of the test (and if the test format allows), go back and review your answers. Be cautious about changing any, since your first instinct tends to be correct, but make sure you didn't misread any of the questions or accidentally mark the wrong answer choice. Look over any you skipped and make an educated guess.

At the end, leave the test feeling confident. You've done your best, so don't waste time worrying about your performance or wishing you could change anything. Instead, celebrate the successful completion of this test. And finally, use this test to learn how to deal with anxiety even better next time.

Review Video: Test Anxiety
Visit mometrix.com/academy and enter code: 100340

Important Qualification

Not all anxiety is created equal. If your test anxiety is causing major issues in your life beyond the classroom or testing center, or if you are experiencing troubling physical symptoms related to your anxiety, it may be a sign of a serious physiological or psychological condition. If this sounds like your situation, we strongly encourage you to seek professional help.

Thank You

We at Mometrix would like to extend our heartfelt thanks to you, our friend and patron, for allowing us to play a part in your journey. It is a privilege to serve people from all walks of life who are unified in their commitment to building the best future they can for themselves.

The preparation you devote to these important testing milestones may be the most valuable educational opportunity you have for making a real difference in your life. We encourage you to put your heart into it—that feeling of succeeding, overcoming, and yes, conquering will be well worth the hours you've invested.

We want to hear your story, your struggles and your successes, and if you see any opportunities for us to improve our materials so we can help others even more effectively in the future, please share that with us as well. **The team at Mometrix would be absolutely thrilled to hear from you!** So please, send us an email (support@mometrix.com) and let's stay in touch.

Online Resources

Due to our efforts to try to keep this book to a manageable length, we've created a link that will give you access to all of your online resources:

mometrix.com/resources719/ssgalitcomp

It's Your Moment, Let's Celebrate It!

Share your story @mometrixtestpreparation